The Modern Alpha Male

A Guide to Masculinity, Women, Money, Assertiveness and Success

Damon Johnson

© **Copyright 2020 - All rights reserved.**

The content contained within this book may not be reproduced, duplicated or transmitted without direct written permission from the author or the publisher.

Under no circumstances will any blame or legal responsibility be held against the publisher, or author, for any damages, reparation, or monetary loss due to the information contained within this book, either directly or indirectly.

Legal Notice:

This book is copyright protected. It is only for personal use. You cannot amend, distribute, sell, use, quote or paraphrase any part, or the content within this book, without the consent of the author or publisher.

Disclaimer Notice:

Please note the information contained within this document is for educational and entertainment purposes only. All effort has been executed to present accurate, up to date, reliable, complete information. No warranties of any kind are declared or implied. Readers acknowledge that the author is not engaged in the rendering of legal, financial, medical or professional advice. The content within this book has been derived from various sources. Please consult a licensed professional before attempting any techniques outlined in this book.

By reading this document, the reader agrees that under no circumstances is the author responsible for any losses, direct or indirect, that are incurred as a result of the use of the information contained within this document, including, but not limited to, errors, omissions, or inaccuracies.

Table of Contents

INTRODUCTION 1
   WHY I CAN HELP YOU 3

CHAPTER 1: THE LARGER THAN LIFE ALPHA MALE 5
   THE REAL QUALITIES 6
   THE ALPHA MALE VARIETY PACK 11
   ALPHA, BETA OR OMEGA? 12
      The Beta Male: 13
      The Omega Male: 14
   THE NEED FOR ALPHAS 14
   BECOMING THE ALPHA 15
      What Would They Do? 16
      Making the Transition: 20

CHAPTER 2: THE NICE GUY SYNDROME 25
   THE CONFUSION AROUND BEING NICE 26
      Nice Guys and Women: 27
   SETBACKS OF BEING A "NICE GUY" 28
      Consequences of Being a Nice Guy: 30
   STOP BEING THE "NICE GUY" 31
      Stop Chasing Validation: 31

CHAPTER 3: ASSERTIVENESS - THE MOST IMPORTANT QUALITY OF THE ALPHA MALE 33
   THE TRUE BENEFITS 34
   WHY DOES ASSERTIVENESS GET A BAD NAME? 36
      Assertiveness vs. Aggressiveness: 37
      Assertiveness vs. Passiveness: 39
      Being Passive-Aggressive: 41
   COMMUNICATING LIKE AN ALPHA 42
      What Else Does Assertiveness Mean: 43
      How to Become Assertive: 44
   PICKING YOUR BATTLES 47

CHAPTER 4: THE LAWS OF ATTRACTION 51

- Law of Attraction History...52
- The Evidence Behind the Law of Attraction.................................54
  - It's Science, Not Fantasy:...55
- Where can the Law of Attraction Help You? 57
- How to use the Law of Attraction 60
  - Decide What You Want:...61
- Law of Attraction Meditation...63
- Why Should Alpha Males Follow This? 64

CHAPTER 5: RECLAIM YOUR MASCULINITY 67

- Masculinity Should Not be Avoided 68
  - What is Masculinity:..70
  - How to Promote Masculinity:..71
- Be a Man, Not a Jerk...71
  - Why Taking Ownership is Beneficial:...73
  - How to Take Ownership: 74
- Creating Your Masculine Edge 75
  - Benefits of the Masculine Edge: 75
  - Steps to Develop Your Masculine Edge: 76
- How to Appear Masculine 80
- Other Concepts of Masculinity..82
  - Actions Speak Louder Than Words:...82
  - Live Your Life Fearlessly:..83
  - Be unreasonable:...85
  - Always Stay Grounded: 85

CHAPTER 6: CONFIDENCE AND LEADERSHIP 87

- Confidence By Category 88
  - External Confidence:..88
  - Internal Confidence: 89
- Living as a Confident Man 91
  - Have a Vision:..91
  - Get to Know Yourself:..92
  - Take Action:...93
  - Be Okay With Failing: 94
  - Confident Men Take Care of Themselves: 95
  - Push Your Boundaries:...95
  - Think Positively:..96
  - Be Generous: 97
  - Ask Questions:...97
  - Don't be a People Pleaser:...98
- Becoming a Confident Man 99
  - 10 Tips to Higher Self-Confidence and Self-Esteem: 99
  - What Confident Men Don't Do:...102

FINDING THE LEADER WITHIN YOU 106
   What Makes a Leader?: *107*
   Learn Leadership: *109*

CONCLUSION 113

REFERENCES 115

Introduction

"The Alpha male does what the other lions fail to do. He reminds himself time and again that he is the Alpha, and second to none."

- Dhanush Bangera

Imagine for a moment, that you are sitting at the bar, watching two different men. They both seem to be interested in the same woman sitting at a nearby table. Most men would find this woman physically attractive and her aloofness adds to her overall mystique. The first man goes to talk to this woman but he has an obviously awkward gait. He hesitates and when he almost reaches the table, he turns around and runs back to the bar. He would love to talk to the woman, but cannot find the courage to do so. As a result, he sits on his stool the whole night alone with his beverage and snacks.

The second man, who also appears interested, walks over to the woman with a confident stride. When he approaches the table, he subtly gets the woman's attention. They begin having a conversation, but you cannot hear what they are saying. By the body language, it appears they are getting along and have some chemistry. After several minutes, the woman gives the man her phone number and he goes back to the bar. Later in the night, the two end up leaving together.

This scenario is a classic example of the differences between an alpha and a beta male. Because the alpha male had courage and confidence, he easily gained the attention and interest of the woman he felt an attraction to. On the other hand, the beta male ended up with nothing because he did not have the same traits. Would the beta male have gained the lady's attention if he approached the table? Probably, but if he would have been awkward like he was while walking to the table, the chances of it going anywhere would be slim to none.

I understand that many gentlemen out there suffer from the safe problem. The lack of self-esteem, confidence and overall masculinity has caused rejection time and again. This occurs not just in the case of finding women, but also getting passed over for promotions at work. In addition, you have probably missed many opportunities for vacations and new adventures. The life you are living is probably not the life you want. I am making a big assumption here, but if you are lacking specific alpha-male qualities, then I am willing to bet that you have a certain fear of going against the grain and instead, live your life based on the wishes of those who are closest to you. You also live your life safely, within the standards of society. I understand this and I want to help you.

This is why I wrote the book, *The Modern Alpha Male*. I want to help you find your own inner alpha and bring him out for the world to see. Once he arrives, your potential to live a life beyond your wildest dreams will increase exponentially. I am not using hyperbole here. Once you shift your mindset from the beta to the alpha male, you will see the world in a whole new light. You will not be afraid to go after what you want and you will not let anything stop you from pursuing your goals, whatever they may be. When you read this book, you will understand fully what a true alpha male is in our modern times.

As you read through the chapters in this book you will learn what real alpha traits are and why you want to pursue them. Unfortunately, the term masculinity has received a negative connotation over the past few years. This book will destroy that idea by describing the positive attributes of being a man and how all of the negative qualities associated with manhood are not actually masculine. In addition to describing what an alpha male is, I will discuss how being a "nice guy" and can leave behind in life. Also, I will detail how the power of the mind through the law of attraction can be used to get what you want. You don't need to be a bully, but understand how to get what you deserve.

I will also delve into the idea of reclaiming your masculinity and its psychological perspective, while also incorporating some physical traits of being a man. Finally, I will round out this book by describing how alpha male traits instill confidence and make a man a great leader, whether he is actually in a leadership role or not.

The overall objective here is to help the men out there, who are not living up to their full potential, find their inner alpha male and begin demanding the life they deserve. You, the reader, will understand that being masculine is not about bullying, manipulating or overpowering people. It is about being a real man. The type of man the world sorely needs at this point. I will guide you in becoming that strong male figure.

Why I Can Help You

I have been talking about the benefits of the book I wrote and I still haven't properly introduced myself. My name is Damon Johnson and I am passionate about helping people reach their full potential. As a boy and a young man growing up, I suffered immensely with low confidence. This made me extremely unhappy, scared, uncomfortable and sometimes, less than human. It was an awful mindset to have because I felt like a prisoner in my own mind. I did not know why I felt this way, but I knew I wanted to change. I had big dreams for myself, and the only way I would reach them was if I became a different person. I heard the phrase, "just be yourself," all the time. Well, if being myself was making me feel the way I did, then myself was not acceptable to me. I was tired of being uncomfortable in my own skin.

I became very interested in psychology, especially in human behavior. By chance, I began studying the psychology of being an alpha male, and slowly, I saw my life changing right before my eyes. The personality of someone who was not an alpha male described me to a "T." As I began learning the theory behind true masculinity and learning the strategies to become a real man, I began incorporating them into my own life. I started with small social interactions and, when I started seeing real results, I became much more intense with my pursuit. I began using the strategies in every aspect of my personal and professional life, and I can happily say that I am a new man. I look in the mirror every day and understand the battle I have to overcome. Being able to live up to my full potential with confidence and fearlessness is a mindset that was once a dream for me. I am happy to say that it is now my reality.

As I watch other men in the same shoes I was once in, I become sick to my stomach. I was once unwanted, overlooked and "friend-zoned" constantly, just like them. It was painful and I never want to see anyone go through that. I could see the real alpha male inside of them, just begging to come out. I know that your alpha male is ready to be released. The information I provide in this book will do just that. My knowledge comes from years of studying and living like the person I hated. I was able to change and I can help you do the same.

If you are willing to read this book from beginning to end and employ its various strategies and techniques, then I assure you that your life will change too. You will finally become the man you need to be, just like I did. If you are ready, then let's get going. I can't wait to see your results!

Chapter 1:

The Larger Than Life Alpha Male

"An alpha male shows others what's possible."

- Asad Meah

"I am the alpha, omega and beta!" Well, if you're like most men, you really are a combination of all three, or solely the last two with no actual alpha male qualities. That is ultimately the man we want to become. The question is: What is a true alpha male and why do so few men actually reach that status?

The alpha male is considered a real man, and rightfully so. He is a man's man and an overall great guy. He is tough when he needs to be and compassion when required. He is strong, but not a bully. He is firm, but not a jerk. He is patient, but not a pushover. You will never be able to take advantage of an alpha male because he will never allow it. The alpha male is socially considered the highest-ranking man in any group that he's in. He is a leader in every way, whether he holds the rank of one or not.

Unfortunately, the term alpha male has received some bad press as of late. Men have been demonized in our society with terms like "toxic masculinity." Violent behavior, bullying and domineering qualities have not helped this cause. What people don't realize is that masculinity and manhood are being mischaracterized by the general population. The negative behaviors that men show, like the ones we just described, are actually not masculine. Therefore, toxic masculinity is an oxymoron. A real man is not supposed to be toxic and, if he is, then he is not showcasing the true attributes of masculinity. He is not an actual alpha male. In this first chapter, I will clear up some of the misconceptions, so that when you hear phrases like, 'being masculine," "manhood," or "alpha male," you will feel a sense of pride, rather than shame.

The Real Qualities

What is a real alpha male like? Believe it or not, it is not that knuckle-dragging meathead at the gym who loves to grunt as he deadlifts whatever amount of weight he is carrying. It is also not that domineering husband who doesn't let his wife get a word in edgewise. Lastly, it is not that guy at the office who acts like he's better than everyone and displays disrespectful behavior towards everybody, especially those who are below him in the hierarchy. These individuals may carry some alpha traits, but they do not encompass the overall alpha personality. The following are some specific traits that make an alpha who he is:

- The alpha male is not a quitter. He is persistent in his goals and will not back down from them. He may reassess, reevaluate and retry, but he will not give up on something he truly wants. This is why he ends up winning in the end.
- The alpha male can defend himself, both with words and his hands. He will not go out and start a fight, but if one comes to him, he will not back down. Along with defending himself, he will defend those close to him.
- The alpha male will keep his mind and body sharp. His diet will consist of nutrient-dense food that is healthy for his brain and will help keep his body in peak physical form. Going to the gym or some type of physical workout will be part of his routine.
- The alpha male is courageous and will face his fears head-on, no matter what they will be.

- The alpha male is not your boring friend who goes to work and then comes home and sits on the couch. He is the guy who goes to the gym prior to work, comes home, and plays a game of basketball, works some more, then takes his wife out to dinner. On his days off, if he has them, he will travel somewhere or try something new. He lives an exciting life and does not strive for average.
- Much to the confusion of many, the alpha male is not arrogant, but actually humble. The courage and confidence can sometimes be taken the wrong way by those who are not used to it. Don't mix up confidence and arrogance. The alpha male will not brag about who he is; he will show you who he is.
- The alpha male is very well-liked. He will often be quiet and reserved but can joke around and have fun with anybody.
- The alpha male has a purpose in life. He is striving for something and will work hard every day to get it.
- The alpha male knows the value of each word and the potential they have to make changes. He does not speak simply to hear his own voice. When he opens his mouth, there is a good reason for it and people will listen.
- The alpha male is an educated man. This does not necessarily mean he has a Ph.D. or even went to college. It simply means he has a thirst for knowledge and never stops learning.
- He does not put others down, but empowers them to succeed. If someone has a dream, even if most think it is outrageous, the alpha male will encourage them to go for it.
- He can converse with anyone, from the bartender to the astrophysicist.
- He is a warrior and not a worrier. He takes action and does what is needed, rather than sitting on his couch fretting about how things will turn out. He does not worry about his future, because he creates it with the work he is doing today.

- The alpha male will not pick a fight with someone. He is not a bully or instigator. If he is ever in a fight, you can be sure he will finish it or die trying.
- The alpha male knows who he is and does not deviate from his values, despite public opinion.
- He respects women and if he has a special one in his life, he will be by her side and help her as much as he can.
- He is willing to help people, but he is not a sucker. He will not allow anyone to run his life and will certainly not go out of his way to please anybody. Like him or don't like him, it doesn't matter.
- He leads by example. There is no, "Do as I say, not as I do," nonsense with the alpha male.
- He does not try to be an alpha male, it's just who he is.
- He knows how to control his emotions. He will get angry, sad, anxious, happy or excited like anyone else, but these emotions will not overtake him. This means that during times of jubilation, people will think he does not care, but during times of crisis, people will love his stoicism. Despite his inner moods, his outward appearance will not change.
- He is decisive! He will make decisions based on what he knows at the time and will take full responsibility for the outcomes.

Based on these attributes, is there anything negative that you see about being an alpha male? These truly characterize what masculinity is all about and those who try to lump aggressive, abusive or arrogant men into this group are grossly misinformed. Consider some of the following fictional stories to help paint a picture of what an alpha male would handle themselves in a real-world setting.

Derek's Story:

Derek has been with his firm for about two years. He is a great worker who is the first to come in and the last to leave. He puts passion into his work and does not waste a lot of time on useless chit-chat. There is an opening for a higher position and Derek knows he is qualified for it. He is fairly sure that he will get the position because of his abilities, confidence and work ethic.

Several other people are vying for the position as well. They are constantly in the boss' office, putting gifts on his desk, acting like his go-fer and buying him lunch. They want the promotion so bad that they are willing to do whatever it takes to get in the boss' good graces. Derek continued to work just as normal, putting in the hours and making sure his results are always superb. While the other employees are bragging about what they've done during the day, Derek just keeps moving without saying much.

When the time comes for the promotion announcement, everyone is anxious to find out who got the job. They all believe they deserve it based on getting the boss to like and notice them. To everyone's surprise, Derek was the chosen one. People were confused because Derek never kissed up to the boss or bragged about all of his accomplishments. He did not have to. All Derek did was come in and do what he was supposed to -- work his butt off to bring in exceptional results. His boss noticed this way more than the people wasting their time trying to manipulate his decision.

Derek's story shows that you don't have to brag or show off who you are, you just have to let your work speak for itself. Derek did not try to change who he was. He did not resort to underhanded tricks to get the boss' attention because he was confident in his results. Even if he didn't get the promotion for whatever reason, he would have continued to work as usual, without a care to what people thought. Derek worked for his own pride and not for the recognition of others, in true alpha male fashion.

Michael's Story:

Michael is a firefighter with five years of experience on the force. He has been involved in many intense situations where he has had to risk his life, just like all of his colleagues. On a recent call, there was a major house fire that quickly engulfed the entire structure. Upon arrival, Michael and a few others ran in to put out the fire as best as they could. The house was not saved, but at least the neighborhood was. They had removed all of the people and animals out of the house, except for one child on the second floor.

Michael reached the room the child was in, but the door was quickly becoming engulfed in flames. He knew that he only had one shot to get in and make it out safely. There was no room for error. While being extremely nervous, Michael took a deep breath then ran in quickly and came out with the child. After this, he immediately ran out of the front door. The child was saved and Michael made it out alive.

When faced with that burning door, Michael showed true alpha qualities. Despite being afraid, he took the initiative and saved that child, which is what being an alpha male is all about. It does not mean having an absence of fear, it is taking action despite fear. Fear can have two meanings:

- Fear Everything And Run *or* Face Everything And Rise. The Alpha male will rise.

Jim's Story:

So, Jim's story is going to be a little different. It will portray the false image of what an alpha male is.

Jim works for a large corporation as an accountant. He is very knowledgeable and was educated at the finest schools, but he is extremely arrogant. People know about all of his accomplishments because he will not hesitate to bring them up. He loves to bemoan and ridicule his colleagues, especially when they ask him for help on something. When he was about to get a new manager, he protested the fact that she was a woman.

When some of his co-workers were talking one morning, Jim interrupted them because he felt his own story was more interesting. Jim always needed to be the center of attention at the office and made sure no one outshined him in any way. If someone was doing good work, Jim would downplay their success, bringing up his own wins in life. The only person who matters to Jim is Jim himself.

Jim is anything but an alpha male. His bullying nature and constant bragging of his own accomplishments do not show any type of confidence. Unfortunately, Jim is the type of man people associate with being an alpha male, rather than Michael or Derek. I am here to change this viewpoint.

The Alpha Male Variety Pack

While there are some foundational characteristics of being an alpha male, there is no single type of alpha. Just like all people, alphas come in different shapes, sizes and types. Each variation has its own unique strengths and characteristics, as well. The business environment is where you will see many alpha style personalities because their attributes often guide them towards winning and competition.

In whatever setting you are in, you have the likelihood of running into one of the following alpha male types. Each one can be a valuable commodity in his own way to help deal with a particular situation. I have provided a brief description for each one:

The Commanders:

These are the magnetic leaders who set the tone for the environment they are in. People are drawn to them because of their attractive personas. These alphas are great at mobilizing the troops, motivating those around them and having an authoritative strength. The commanders are great in leadership roles and will often be seen as the leaders, even if they don't officially hold the rank.

If you have worked for a business, you may have had a manager who was given the role of a leader but did not have the traits to back up their title. As a result, someone else in the office, who was lower in the hierarchy, becomes the unofficial leader. This dynamic occurs often when people are natural leaders mixed in with others who are simply followers.

The Visionaries:

These alphas are curious, innovative, intuitive and future-oriented. They see opportunities and possibilities that others don't and are very proactive in making them happen. They are not just dreamers, but doers. While some individuals will dismiss visionary alphas as impractical, others will be inspired by their drive. If a visionary has talents in engineering and art, but only a passion for the latter, you can bet he will work to become an artist. Or, he might try to combine the two.

The Strategists:

These alphas are systematic, methodical and brilliant thinkers. They are drawn to data and facts and the actions they take are done for a particular purpose. They will never be the reactionary types. They move forward strategically with a plan in mind.

The Executors:

The alphas are the goal-oriented doers who trudge forward and make things happen. They are extremely disciplined and never let obstacles get in their way. They are detail-oriented and will hold people accountable for what they do or say. If you tell an executor alpha that you are going to do something, then you better get it done somehow.

All of these types will play a significant role in a business setting as all of their characteristics and talents will provide extreme benefits to any organization. There are a lucky few alphas in this world who possess the attributes of all of these individuals.

Alpha, Beta or Omega?

Not every man can be an alpha male. If you are reading this book, I am willing to bet that you are more of a beta or omega as far as your dominant traits are concerned. This does not mean you are a bad man, but the qualities you possess are much less appealing to other people. Also, you are much less likely to reach your goals and live a life that makes you happy, if you fall under the beta or omega umbrella. I will briefly go over what these two male types are so you can get an idea of where you are and where you need to be.

The Beta Male:

Beta males will display a mild level of confidence, but for the most part, will be unsure of themselves. They will usually follow the lead of an alpha, even if they hold a higher position than they do. Any beta male will lack the confidence to lead other men or women. As a result, he will never go on his own path and create his own life. He will always live the life that society thinks he deserves.

Beta males often miss out on hooking up with women and are often "friend-zoned." This is especially true when an alpha male is around. A woman will see the alpha male as a confident man who is difficult to get and a beta male as low-hanging fruit she can pick any time. She may respect the beta to a certain degree, but will be less sexually attracted to him.

A beta male will try excessively hard to please people, whether at work or among his friends. He will have a hard time saying no because he fears it will upset somebody. As a result, people will ask him for favors constantly and keep pushing the limits to see what they can get away with. While an alpha male would stop someone dead in their tracks if they jumped over the boundaries, a beta male had no real boundaries in the first place. Whatever is your wish will become his desire.

The ironic thing is, the qualities that are often associated with alpha males, like brashness and arrogance, are actually beta traits. Many betas will talk about their accomplishments and make it obvious to others what they have done. The reason for this is to hide their insecurities and lack of confidence. Most people can see right through them.

The Omega Male:

One notch below the beta male is the omega male. These individuals suffer from very low self-confidence and they cannot hide it. He will be plagued with extreme nervousness and have a high fear in social settings. These types of men are neither leaders nor second in command. If there is an alpha or beta present, he will follow one of them.

While betas can fake being confident to a degree, an omega has no shot at this because his insecurities are way too strong to hide. This is the man who gets walked over constantly and never stands up for himself. He is a perpetual victim. Even others with low confidence think he is weak.

At work, the omega rarely gets noticed. When he does, it's because someone wants a favor from him, and they know he will do it with no pushback. He will never ask for what's rightly his, because he is too afraid and often feels he doesn't deserve it.

When it comes to women, they will try to use the "innocent guy" approach in hopes to be given a chance, at the very least. A good woman will leave this guy alone, while a bad woman will take complete advantage and make him do her bidding. While a woman could see a beta male as a friend, an omega would not even be allowed near her for long periods, because she will not respect him in any way. The omega male is the ultimate cowardly man. If you find yourself in this camp, then there's a lot of work to be done.

The Need for Alphas

The goal of being an alpha male is to be the type of man other men respect, and women want to be with. Betas and omegas are seen as the nice guys, which we will get more into during the next chapter.

People often associate lifestyles and viewpoints with being either strong or weak. For example, men who are part of the LGBTQ community are often seen as weak and ineffective, while big burly looking men who live out in the country are seen as tough. As you can see from the descriptions, being an alpha male has nothing to do with sexual orientation, lifestyle, political persuasion or background. It is how they carry themselves, treat others and believe in who they are. There are skinny male hairdressers who are more alpha than many MMA fighters. Being an alpha male is not about what you do, it's who you are.

Unfortunately, at a time when we need alphas more than ever, there seems to be a large group of men becoming betas and omegas. Unfortunately, a big reason is because many men are confused. In modern times, little boys are being indoctrinated from a young age to avoid characteristics that are inherently masculine. They are told to tone down their behavior, be less aggressive, not to roughhouse and even become submissive. Essentially, they are taught that it's wrong to be a boy.

Let me clarify something. Boys have a natural tendency to be aggressive and this can lead to them becoming violent if not managed properly. However, teaching a boy to control his behaviors to help him channel his emotions is vastly different than making him feel ashamed about being a male.

Becoming the Alpha

Since society needs alpha males, it is time to transition from being a beta or omega, if you fall under those categories. The first step to making a change is admitting that you have a problem that needs to be fixed. Before getting into the action steps, I want you to assess yourself objectively and determine if you are, indeed, an alpha, beta or omega, based on the descriptions above. If you see yourself as a beta or omega, then it's time to get to work. If you honestly see yourself as an alpha, then you can still proceed because there will always be room for improvement. This is the mindset of an alpha male, anyway.

What Would They Do?

You may have noticed that many individuals end up on different paths in life, even though they have the same background. Yes, there are many factors at play, but a major one is how you approach the world. Those who live their lives with a winning attitude do actually win more. If you want to win too, then begin thinking and behaving like winners. I will show you how.

In this section, I want to further emphasize the difference between an alpha, beta and omega man by detailing how each of them would handle a hypothetical situation. Based on the individual personality traits, the actions used will be vastly different. I will use the same scenario throughout to maintain consistency and to fully showcase the varying personalities. While the story is not real, it will thoroughly illustrate the varying results you can achieve, just by having different personality traits.

The Alpha at a Party:

After arriving at a party at a friend's house, James looked around for a while and acknowledged a few people with eye contact. He then went to find his friend. He noticed him talking to someone, so he grabbed a few snacks from the table while waiting. He was enjoying the treats while observing what was going on.

In the meantime, he also struck up a conversation with a woman who was also standing by the snack table. While James was friendly and conversive, he allowed her to do the majority of the talking, while occasionally asked followup questions. He was interested in learning more about her and remained somewhat aloof about his own life. However, he was happy to bring things up if he was asked but just did not divulge anything extra.

After about 10 minutes, James and the woman, whose name was Michelle, seemed to be interested in each other. When James saw his friend walking over, he politely told Michelle that he had to go, but said he would like to speak with her another time. He asked Michelle for her number, and she gave it to him. After the interaction, they both went their separate ways. James began talking to his friend, who promptly asked him about the girl. James simply told him that she was someone he met and had a conversation with. After this, he moved on to avoid bragging about the situation.

The next day, after getting some of his work done, James found Michelle's number and gave her a quick call. She did not answer, so he left her a message and waited for her response. Several hours later, Michelle did call him back and they had another great conversation. There seemed to be a good amount of chemistry, so James asked her to meet him the following night at one of his favorite restaurants. Michelle agreed and the date was set.

In James' story, he displayed confidence in how he carried himself. He never bragged or made himself feel more important than anyone else. The fact that he didn't call Michelle excessively or follow her around at the party showed that he had dignity and was not insecure about himself.

James displayed alpha qualities throughout the entire exchange.

The Beta at a Party:

Tom went to his friend's house for a party. Right after he drove up, he spent about five minutes looking into his mirror to make sure his hair was perfect. After stepping out of the car, he spent another minute making sure his jacket was straight. When he entered the house, he walked around nervously, making subtle eye contact with some of the people around him. He was trying not to bring too much attention to himself.

Once he located his friend, he started walking up to say "Hi." His friend was in the middle of a conversation. Tom tried to get his attention from afar, but it didn't work. Eventually, he walked over to the snack table. There were a few people there, so he sheepishly walked up and just grabbed a couple of finger foods. He was still trying not to get noticed.

Tom's friend was still talking to another guest, so he decided to stand up against the wall, hoping to blend into the background. There was a young woman standing nearby. Tom was looking at her, but she did not seem to notice him. He kept on glancing over at her nervously but did not have the guts to speak up. He came close a few times, but then just shut down and retreated back to his corner.

Eventually, as Tom glanced over at her, she made eye contact with him. Tom just shot over a nervous grin. She gave him a half-smile then turned back around. He became even more nervous at this point but figured the smile might have meant something. Before she could walk away, Tom hesitantly told her his name. The woman turned around and told him that her name was Michelle.

Tom really had no idea where to go from here. He thought Michelle was attractive, but could not get any words out. After some fidgeting, he was able to blurt out, "I live around the corner. How about you?"

Michelle told him that she lived nearby as well. Tom continued to stand against the wall, searching for his next words. After a few moments, he said, "Well, maybe I'll see you around then."

Michelle turned around and responded, "Yes, maybe." After some more awkward silence, Michelle eventually excused herself. Tom gave her a wave. He wanted to ask Michelle for her number but was too scared. After she left, Tom took a deep breath and started lightly hitting his head against the wall. When his friend walked up, he asked Tom who the woman was, but Tom just shrugged it off without answering.

If you noticed in both of the stories, there was nothing mentioned about the physical attractiveness in both men. Honestly, that is subjective anyway. Also, it is not important to the circumstances. Tom, the beta male, would not have been able to hook up with Michelle, whether she found him attractive or not. His lack of confidence was obvious and it likely turned Michelle off too.

Confidence and how you carry yourself is key to getting what you want in life. This is not only relatable to getting a date. It goes for getting anything you want in life and living as you choose, despite what people think of you. There was a chance that James would have been shot down by Michelle, but he would have just moved on. If Tom built up the courage to ask Michelle on a date and got shot down, he would have been devastated. Just for fun, we will portray the same scenario with an omega male.

The Omega at a Party:

Jesse arrived at his friend's house for a party. As he pulled up, he noticed several people standing around. He decided to wait until most of them went inside before getting out of his car. Once the coast cleared up a little, Jesse got out and slowly began walking towards the door. He tried to dodge people as he kept his head down.

Once Jesse walked in, he became overwhelmed by the crowd. He did not know where to go. He could not find his friend and did not want to go looking for him through all of the people. He noticed a snack bar, so he quickly went over to get some food. When other party-goers got to the snacks first, Jesse just hung back and waited for them to leave. Then, Jesse quickly filled up his plate.

After getting the snacks he wanted, Jesse looked over and saw a woman standing by the table, who looked pretty attractive. He had no intention of walking up to her, though. He decided to find a seat in the corner so that he could stay isolated from everybody else. Eventually, his friend found him and encouraged him to walk around and mingle with people. Jesse tried to do this, but after a while, he snuck out of the party and drove home while his friend was talking to someone else.

As an Omega, Jesse is the epitome of a weak man. He has no confidence and is extremely anxious in any social setting. If you are an omega or a beta, the goal is to transition into an alpha, so you can be the ultimate man who lives life on his own terms. We were all created individually, so no one else understands us better than we do. It is our job to determine what kind of life we want to live and how.

The reason people remain betas and omegas is that they are terrified of standing out from the crowd. Their self-consciousness prevents them from living with the alpha mindset. Now that you know the benefits, it is time to let that inner alpha out. He has been suffocating long enough, and he needs an opportunity to breathe. I will warn you, though, once your alpha sees the light, he will not want to go back in, which is a great thing. If you're ready, let's start shifting that mindset.

Making the Transition:

There's the old expression that blonds have more fun. Well, this statement holds true for alpha males, as well. They have fun because they choose to make their lives fun. Have you always been jealous of people who are living their best life? Well, you can start living the same way.

Many modern men have lost their backbone and the desire to be, well, men. Instead of standing up for what they believe in, they have been reduced to following the status quo. They would rather live their entire lives longing for something better, than standing up and pissing a few people off.

To those of thinking it's just for more money, sex, fun or prestige, it is actually about none of those. These are just byproducts. More than anything, it is about living a life of freedom, where you will have no regrets in the end. The beta male ends up living his life in quiet desperation. This is the opposite of an alpha male, who lives with satisfaction.

As you begin your transition to an alpha male, you will begin noticing changes right away. Life will just seem better and you will be happier. One thing to remember is that alphas are constantly working on themselves to maintain and build their masculinity. I don't want you to think that once you've made the transition, that all of your work is done. Working on yourself will never be completed. To become the alpha male you are hoping for, you must adopt the following traits:

Become More Assertive:

Some men tell you exactly what they think, while others beat around the bush, hoping you will pick up on what they're saying. People are not mind-readers, and if you want them to know what you're thinking, you need to tell them respectfully, but firmly. For example, if a friend asks you to go out for the night but you can't go, then you must tell them that directly. If they push back, then you must stand firm. If you give in even a little bit, then you've lost. If you can't go out or don't want to go out, then you don't go out.

Also, you do not owe your friends any explanation as to why. You simply decline politely, then end the conversation. If they ask, tell them again that you can't and that's it. "No" is a complete sentence. I will get into the topic of assertiveness more thoroughly in a later chapter.

Accept Change:

Alphas will always accept changes they have no control over and work to adapt the best they can to the new circumstances. If alphas need to change to better themselves, then they will actively work on doing so. They take full responsibility for their lives and do not sit around and complain about what is happening to them.

I want you to understand right now that you cannot control everything that happens to you. However, you can learn and then move forward. You ultimately decide how you will react to something. In the end, the life you build will be based on the choices that you make. Next time you are faced with a challenge, like losing a job, do not sit around whining about it. This is a complete waste of time and won't solve your problem. Figure out why you lost your job and begin looking for new ones every chance you get. Also, focus on things you can improve on, like your resume, the way you communicate and certain skills that are lacking. If you focus on the solution, rather than the problem, you will make a lot of positive progress.

Be a Gentlemen, not a Nice Guy:

Alpha males are courteous, polite, considerate and kind to everyone, as long as they get the same treatment in return. Alphas put their needs before anyone else's. This is not because they are selfish, but because they respect themselves enough to know they deserve it. While an alpha will treat others well, they will not become a doormat for anybody.

The key difference between an alpha gentleman and a beta nice guy is their motivation for how they act. Alphas are kind because it is the right thing to do. They feel good when they are kind to others. Betas, on the other hand, treat others well because they desperately seek their approval. As a result, no matter how a beta nice guy is treated by another person, they will continue to be nice, because they don't want to upset anyone. An alpha gentleman realizes that when someone treats them poorly, they have lost all rights to kindness. I will cover nice guys more in Chapter 2.

If you want to be an alpha, you must stop caring about the approval of others. Treat people kindly and be there for them, if they deserve it. This means to be courteous, kind and respectful. If you get the same treatment back, continue being this way. If you get disrespect back, then you are no more Mr. Nice Guy. You don't have to start a fight, but you need to dismiss the person from your life.

Seek Genuine Connections, not Validation:

A common theme in this book has been that alphas do not need validation. They don't talk to people because they are trying to get their attention or get something from them. They desire genuine connections where they meet someone they can get along with on a personal level. This is true, whether it is a romantic partner or friend.

Do not put people, men or women, on pedestals. Treat them as equals and do your best to create a strong bond that brings value to both individuals.

Trust Yourself:

Alphas look for solutions to life's problems within themselves. This is because they trust themselves and know they have the ability to succeed in this manner. While they might seek out advice and guidance along the way, they do not rely on other people to fix their problems. The alpha male will make up his mind based on what he knows best about himself.

Strive for Growth:

Alphas give their best in every situation, no matter how minor it may seem. They do not settle for mediocrity and will always strive for excellence. Also, their desire for growth is not to impress others, but to satisfy their own pride in who they are.

Face Your Demons:

Alpha males are not perfect people who have no problems. They have weaknesses, just like the rest of us. The difference is they do not hide from them. They confront their demons head-on because they know that is the only way to overcome them. This goes along with seeking constant growth.

Communicate with Clarity and Respect:

When an alpha male needs to communicate something, he is respectful, clear and firm. He speaks his mind then listens appropriately for the response. He is total class all the way and does not throw tantrums to seek attention. Alpha males negotiate and persuade to get what they want, while beta males pout, cry and make a scene. Their ability to communicate is poor, just like many other qualities about them. The alpha knows how to communicate and, therefore, gets what he wants

If you want to become an alpha, then you must start following the traits I just went over. You can no longer be that pushover who is just trying to survive. You must become the lion who lives life on his own terms.

Chapter 2:

The Nice Guy Syndrome

"Just because you are a nice guy, doesn't mean you are a good man."

- Zyanya Torres

I am not trying to imply that being nice equates to being bad. I just want to debunk that idea that to be a good man, you always have to be nice to everyone. In fact, sometimes you have to be anything but nice to let people know not to mess with you.

Unfortunately, many guys out there are confused about their role. They were told over and over again that manliness is a negative quality. As a result, many males began acting feminine, but they were ridiculed for this as well. To compromise, they simply chose the nice guy personality to avoid drama and conflict. Now there are many men out there who are excessively nice, thinking that it's the only way they can be. The bad part is, they are not genuinely nice, but act in that manner to survive or get what they want.

There is a phenomenon out there known as the Nice Guy Syndrome. When a man is plagued with this, he goes about his life trying to be as neutral as possible, because he feels that it is the best way to live. He never rocks the boat, never challenges anyone, never questions anything and certainly never calls a person out. Even if he has been wronged in his life, he just carries on and never disavows the people involved in any way. He may even allow the disrespectful person to treat him in the same manner continuously, thinking his niceness will eventually win the day.

The "nice guy" is generally agreeable with other people, no matter how insane their beliefs are. He tries his best to never upset anybody, so he will go out of his way to make others happy. He wants to be everyone's friend, despite how they treat him. A man like this lives with the assumption that his life will always be fun, happy and drama-free. This is a false assumption. If anything, they will have more of these things because they allow them into their lives.

"Nice guys" have many issues to deal with, the majority of which are inside their own heads. If you are a nice guy, then you know exactly what I am talking about. People with these personalities will always have conflicts in their minds about what they should do and what they will actually do. Unfortunately, they can never make that mind-body connection, so their actions and behaviors are generally the opposite of what they are thinking. In summary, they are not living life how they want to, but how others want them to. They care more about validation, than actually being happy.

The Confusion Around Being Nice

If you ask most people if being "nice" is a positive character trait, most will answer in the affirmative. However, there are negative characteristics of being a nice guy that go beyond what I already mentioned above. Dr. Robert Glover, who is considered an authority on Nice Guy Syndrome" and the author of, *No More Mr. Nice Guy: A Proven Plan for Getting What You Want in Love, Sex and Life,* describes a more sinister agenda that is out there. "Nice guys" are not always being nice for the sake of helping someone. In some cases, this may be true, and I certainly don't want to indict everyone. However, if you notice a man who is excessively nice to everyone, it might behoove you to question some of his motives.

Many guys out there have learned that being nice will allow them to get what they want from people, especially women. They will play the game by doing something, or many things nicely, then expect something equally as kind done for them. In the case of women, this could be a manipulation tactic to extract a sexual favor later on. They will think they are entitled to something like this automatically after doing something kind. In regard to other relationships, like work, friends, or family, nice guys will use their kindness specifically to catch people off guard. Rather than asking for what they want directly, as an alpha would, they will strategically do nice things for others to soften them up and then ask for favors because they know they have some leverage over them. Doing something kind for another person, while expecting something in return, is not true kindness.

Nice Guys and Women:

There have been many different studies down throughout the years regarding how "nice guys" are perceived by women. Of course, there was no uniform result during these studies since desirability factors in men are completely dependent on individual women. Each female has her own opinion on what makes a good man.

For example, a 2008 study in Las Cruces, New Mexico, at New Mexico State University, showed that "nice guys" reported far fewer sexual partners. A 2010 study done by Barclay found that men who performed generous acts seemed more desirable for long-term relationships. Many women have reported the "nice guy" as committed and respectful, while others found him to be boring and lacking in confidence. The author of the 2010 study suggests that being nice is a quality that women look for in men, but this trait is often carried by men who are less attractive in other areas, like physical appearance or personality. Therefore, some men use niceness to compensate for other qualities they lack. So, is the "nice guy" in this respect truly nice, or just pretending to be to get by? There is no simple answer here, but the research suggests the latter.

What we need to focus on is being a good man and a good man is definitely nice to people, but not necessarily a "nice guy" in regards to being manipulative or a pushover.

Setbacks of Being a "Nice Guy"

I will start this section by giving you two different scenarios. These will illustrate how a "nice guy" conducts himself in various situations and what the results are.

Nick's Story:

Nick works as a computer programmer and he is absolutely brilliant in his work. He graduated from a top university and can accomplish almost any task with ease. When something is harder to figure out, Nick will put in the extra effort needed to work through it. He is probably the best person at his job. When a promotion opens up, Nick would be the obvious choice, but he is actually in competition with another individual, who is less talented, but more assertive and confident.

Nick is a very diminutive guy, who will even do other people's work for them, and allow them to have all the credit. This includes the individual he is in competition with. Since Nick is a nice guy and does not want to upset anyone, whenever he is asked to take on an extra load by this co-worker, he does so without even putting up a fight. When the boss is close to announcing a promotion, Nick remains quiet, while his co-worker explains all of the accomplishments he has had. While doing so, he explains in a clear and concise manner why he would do great in the new role. He is not nearly as competent, skilled or hardworking as Nick, but because he is more confident, he is given the promotion. Nick is left in his current role, continuing to be a "nice guy" who does not get what he wants.

Nick represents a "nice guy" who is a good person, but he allows his niceness to become a weakness. In the first place, he should not be doing other people's work without receiving the credit and he should not be overlooked for a promotion because he is too afraid to ask for what he wants. Nick deserves better than this.

Mike's Story:

Mike works in an office with many different people. One day, his co-worker, Tonya, is given a project that is very complicated. Being a "nice guy," Mike decides to help her. He literally stays at work for several hours every day for several days to help Tonya. She really appreciates his help. By Friday night, they complete the project. At this time, Mike askes Tonya if she wants to grab a drink at a bar nearby. Tonya, who appreciates Mike's kindness, agrees and they go out to get some appetizers and drinks.

While sitting at the table, Mike and Tonya talk and get to know each other, as they know very little about each other outside of work. After finishing a couple of drinks, Mike asks Tonya to come back to his place. Tonya, who is confused by this, respectfully declines. Mike looks over at her bewildered and then goes into a rage. He cannot believe she is declining his request after all he had done for her.

Tonya became even more upset by this and started to leave. Mike was cursing her out for using him to get her way. This is ironic, because Mike was actually using her, not the other way around.

Mike's story is an example of a "nice guy" using his kindness as a way to be manipulative. He did not help Tonya because he was being genuine, but because he was expecting something in return. Tonya never even asked Mike for help. He offered it and, in his mind, the effort he put in was futile. Tonya will have a greater distrust in men because of this interaction. From now on, she will always question their motives.

An alpha male would have never been caught in any of these scenarios. At least, not more than once. He would have worked hard and been knowledgeable, like Nick, but he would have never taken a back seat to anyone or done other people's work for them. He would have set some strict boundaries. Also, he would have helped Tonya to a degree, but not to the point where it would have impacted his time in a major way. Also, he would not have expected anything in return.

Consequences of Being a Nice Guy:

If you haven't noticed by now, "nice guys" do not have the most desirable qualities, and they don't live enjoyable lives, because they are too busy being overly kind to other people. There are many consequences of being a "nice guy" and the following are some of the major ones.

An Unsatisfying Dating Life:

"Nice guys" will not be able to get the dates they want with the women they want because they will be too pursuant and overly kind in their efforts. While women don't dislike "nice guys," they want someone who is a little hard to get. Someone who is always at their beck and call, even before they really know them, is a huge turnoff and even a little creepy. Also, as we saw in the example above, it could indicate some ulterior motive. Even if that is not your angle, many women will assume this, especially those who have experienced it in the past.

If a "nice guy" does find a woman, he could lose her quickly by being too clingy. He will always want to be around her and never respect her personal space. She will become turned off and move on, while you will be left sulking in your tears.

Poor Friendships:

A "nice guy" will not have any real friends. A lot of the people around him will use him for their own benefits. The "nice guy" will realize this only when the friends leave him because he can no longer serve their purposes. Unfortunately, many "nice guys" will not learn their lessons and keep surrounding themselves with the same kinds of people.

Treadmill Existence:

This is a phenomenon when a person lives the same existence over and over again. This is because they have underlying feelings of hopelessness. This includes running back to the same people who cause you misery.

A Mediocre Life:

The "nice guys" are not the ones taking risks, trying new things or living the life they want. "Nice guys" are not able to assert themselves in a certain direction and, therefore, like an average life with an okay job, living paycheck to paycheck and just trying to coast through life. You will exist, but not really live.

As you can see, living as a "nice guy" is not the most appealing type of existence. It's time to break the chain of living in this manner.

Stop Being the "Nice Guy"

To become the alpha male, you must break your familiar patterns of being a nice guy. You can do this, no matter how long you have been living this way. Nice guys do finish last in many respects and it's time for you to charge to the front. The following are some strategies to help you stop being a "nice guy."

Stop Chasing Validation:

The core need for a "nice guy" is to achieve validation through whatever means necessary. The more validation you get, the more you need. Eventually, it takes power over you. I am not saying that it doesn't feel good to get recognized. It is okay to accept compliments in a graceful way. Just don't let it take over your life.

In order to stop this cycle, you just have to stop doing things for other people's praise. Next time you take a trip, stop being so eager to post about it on social media. In fact, take a trip alone that nobody knows about and just have a good time. This goes for any other action you take in life. Just do it and don't explain it to anyone. The more you do things along without telling people, the more you will realize that their validation is not important in your life.

Start Saying "No" With Assertiveness:

When you start saying "no" without being meek, it will show that you mean what you say. Saying this word is hard because "nice guys" like to be people pleasers. Stop behaving in this fashion by realizing that this is your life, and you are not responsible for other people's happiness. You are responsible for yours and they are responsible for theirs. Assertiveness will be a major topic of discussion in the next chapter.

Stop Following the Rules:

"Nice guys" are often sticklers for following the rules of society because they are afraid to go beyond the social constructs of life. I am not telling you to do anything illegal here. There are universal rules that all people must follow. However, you are not bound to the limitations that people put on you. You do not have to follow some set path. You are allowed to create your own rules once in a while and start living your life with your own passion.

Life is chaotic in nature and no matter how much you stick to the rules, you are going to be bumped off the road on occasion. Life is not predictable, so it's better to create your own blueprint for making yourself happy. Follow the trailblazers, as they are the ones who made history.

On a final note, aim to be authentic and not just "nice." Authenticity means you are being your true self. So, if you are nice to someone, it's because you genuinely want to be.

Chapter 3:

Assertiveness - The Most Important Quality of the Alpha Male

Consider these two separate statements:
- "Um, I am not sure if I can do this. Can someone help me? If not, it's okay. I don't want to bother anybody."
- "I am unsure of how to proceed here. Before I continue, I will need some answers and assistance."

Both of these statements portray a sense of uncertainty, however, one person is meekly asking for help, not knowing if they will get it or not. Meanwhile the other person makes his feelings clear and lets us know what his expectations are. Either he will get the assistance he needs or he is not pushing forward. Neither statement is rude, but one of them definitely holds more strength than the other. This is because it shows some assertiveness.

Assertiveness is a mode of communication where a person expresses themselves with clarity, confidence and firmness while maintaining a respectful attitude. When a man converses in this manner, he is completely sure of himself and other people will know that he means what he says. Speaking with assertiveness is a great way to express your point of view and stand up for what you believe in, without coming off as rude and obnoxious. If you cannot communicate in this manner, then no one will take you seriously. In fact, you are not taking yourself seriously.

Being assertive is the most important quality an alpha male can have. This is because communication is the ultimate way that a person can convey what they want. The more assertively a man speaks, the more likely his message will get across. As a result, he is more likely to get what he asked for. Alpha males build the life they want because they are not afraid to ask for it with confidence.

If you want to become an alpha male, then assertiveness is a skill that you must develop, without question. Assertiveness equates to confidence. This will be the focus of this chapter.

The True Benefits

Becoming an assertive man brings a lot of value to your life. The objective is to keep a balance between not being submissive while avoiding becoming dominant. When you are submissive, you are always the one who compromises. When you are dominant, you are never willing to compromise with anyone else. I understand that some situations in life will require you not to budge. However, in the overall scheme of things, you will have to give a little at a time, while getting a little at other moments. A healthy level of assertiveness is what we are after.

Assertiveness is closely related to self-confidence. As you build your skills to be assertive, your confidence level goes up, and vice versa. Both of these skills are essential to obtaining any level of success in life. Once you are competent in these areas, you will improve upon your decision-making skills; recognize your strengths and weaknesses; be able to tune in to your real feelings; and become focused and determined on making your life positive.

A bonus here is that once you've added value to your life, you can also help other people. A self-confident person has no problem reaching down and helping someone else up. They are never threatened by anyone's ambition because they believe in themselves. People will pick up on your positive energy and feel good about who they are too.

The following are some other benefits to being assertive. As you will see, it makes you a better man in every way.

- We already covered the communication benefits, but just to reinforce, you will communicate more effectively, which will lead to more career success, better relationships and an ability to handle difficult situations by having clear conversations.
- You will build up your self-esteem. Research shows that people who are assertive tend to honor their values more. Self-esteem is different from self-confidence. Self-confidence refers to being sure of yourself in certain situations, while self-esteem means you have high self-worth overall.
- Being assertive helps you get what you want, which means you start believing that you have the competence to reach your goals. As a result, you will have more positive thoughts, which will further lead to positive outcomes.
- You are more likely to achieve your goals. Once you set a goal, you will have the capability of expressing your needs clearly, which will help you reach your goals.
- You will make better friends because you will be your authentic self. You will have no doubt that the people in your life genuinely like you for who you are, and not for some fake persona. You will weed out fake friends who do cross that barrier.
- Assertiveness makes you more likable because people know what you want and don't have to guess, which is annoying and unflattering.
- Assertiveness leads to reduced social anxiety because we are not concerned about upsetting people.

An assertive man is a more competent man in every sense of the imagination. It can be nerve-racking to be assertive, especially if you're used to being passive. I admit, it may take a while to transition, but it will be worth it in the end.

Why Does Assertiveness Get a Bad Name?

With all of the beneficial qualities that assertiveness has, why does it get such a bad reputation? A lot of this has to do with misconception, just like being an alpha male does. People often misconstrue assertiveness with being mean, rude or arrogant. The words are used interchangeably too by some individuals, which does not help. It is important to clearly define what assertiveness is, and how it is actually much different from the negative traits associated with it.

Assertive communication or behavior is based on having mutual respect for each other. The style is firm, yet diplomatic in nature. It does not involve yelling, name-calling or pettiness. It is a straightforward and highly effective way to get your message across. When you speak in an assertive manner, it showcases that you have a passion for what you are talking about. The fact that the overall tone still remains respectful also demonstrates that you are aware of the other person and their right to have an opinion.

Assertive communication is by far the best type of communication because it is direct and clear. The person on the receiving end will not feel like they're getting attacked or dominated but will understand that the other individual means business. The excuse of miscommunication will not be viable here. This is what true assertiveness is. Unfortunately, this is not how it is represented in the public sphere on so many occasions. I am here to change that, by finally deciphering between assertive, aggressive and passive speech.

Assertiveness vs. Aggressiveness:

While assertive behavior is firm and direct, it is not aggressive. Although, this is how it often gets interpreted. Being assertive has nothing to do with being mean or bullying someone. The person communicating in this fashion still maintains an aura of respect. Aggressive communication, on the other hand, goes way over the top. The person displaying this behavior is practically in your face and has total disregard for your opinion. He is not there to converse but to demand. He has no plans on negotiating and just wants everything done his way.

Men who are aggressive are definitely bullies who believe they are more important than those around them. While an assertive person will handle things diplomatically, the aggressive person uses intimidation, humiliation or manipulation. They will resort to name-calling and maybe even physical violence. These individuals think they are acting tough, but in reality, they are showcasing deep insecurities. They know they can't argue their point, so they try to force people to do what they want.

Aggression undercuts any type of trust or mutual respect. If you constantly show aggressive behavior, people will resent you, avoid you or even oppose you, which will just escalate the situation. Being aggressive might get you what you want in certain circumstances, but you will lose in the end. The goal of aggressive behavior is to win, whether you are right or wrong. The goal of assertive behavior is to find a balance between different ideas.

The following are some examples of assertive and aggressive communication to further illustrate the difference. I will start with the assertive conversation first.

- Person 1: "I think we need to try a different method of distributing projects fairly."
- Person 2: "That's an interesting point. Why do you feel that way?"

- Person 1: "Well, many tasks are not getting completed and some of the employees are complaining about doing more work than others without extra pay."
- Person 2: "That's definitely something we need to look into. However, before we make any drastic changes, we should further assess the situation and make sure the problems we are dealing with are crystal clear."
- Person 1: "That is definitely a good idea."
- Person 2: "Great! We will begin working on the assessments this afternoon to determine the problems and then come up with solutions by the end of the week."

The communication here was direct, respectful, clear, and concise. Nobody said more than they needed to and thoroughly listened to what the other person had to say. In the end, both individuals got their point across and came to a resolution. This is a simple example of assertive communication but makes the point that it is not rude or aggressive in any way. It is basically how a normal conversation should go.

I will now present the same type of conversation, but with an aggressive tone.

- Person 1: "You know, I am getting sick of the way things are getting done around here."
- Person 2: "What's your problem? Please be more specific."
- Person 1: "Well, some of us are working our butts off, while others won't get off their butts."
- Person 2: "Who are these other people you are referring to?"
- Person 1: "The lazy employees. You know what I'm talking about."
- Person 2: "That better not be a shot at me! Who are you, Mr. Work-a-holic?"
- Person 1: "Compared to you, yes." (At this point, Person 2 gets in his face).

- Person 2: "You've got some nerve! Who do you think you are? Everything is fine the way it is."
- Person 1: "Okay, whatever you say, bro!"
- Person 2: "Why don't you just get out of here?"
- Person 1: "Why don't you make me?"

As you can see, this conversation escalated very quickly. It started off with some mild aggression and resulted in a major confrontation. This scenario can go in several different ways. Either one or both men might back down and retreat from further issues. Another person watching the confrontation might step in and prevent any major problems. Or it could result in a physical confrontation.

The communication was disrespectful from the beginning. It was met with an equal amount of disrespect and resulted in both individuals becoming heated. The initial problem did not get resolved and, in fact, it was not clear what the issue was. This happens often with aggressive communication, which shows it is clearly deficient compared to assertive communication.

Assertiveness vs. Passiveness:

Many people believe that passiveness is a better route to take than assertiveness due to the fact that they see assertive behavior as too aggressive. As we described earlier, assertiveness and aggressiveness are vastly different. So, how does assertive communication compare to passive behavior? While assertive people stand up for themselves and make their requests clearly known, passive individuals just go with the flow and do not want to rock the boat, even a little bit. They hate confrontation and will never speak up about their feelings, no matter how deep they are.

The problem with passive people is that they are too nice. People completely disregard their feelings, mainly because they have no clue what they are. Even if they express their emotions, it's done in a way that makes no impact. As a result, they are not taken seriously and get walked all over. Passiveness is usually practiced by omega males, and some beta males too, who are considered weak overall.

Passiveness is basically you conforming to the world around you in every way and never putting up any type of fight. This means that whenever someone asks you about anything, you immediately agree with them, despite how much you disagree, or don't want to do what they are asking. As a result, you put up with things no one should ever have to deal with. If you are a passive person, then you probably notice yourself being busy all the time. This is not because you are working on your goals, but because you are running around taking care of everyone else. Why are you required to do this, especially if the person is capable of doing it themselves? The answer is, you are not.

Here are some examples of passive communication.

- Your boss asks you to stay late at work for a last-minute project that he could assign to someone else, but you have dinner plans with your wife. Instead of politely declining, you meekly say "yes." Now you have to cancel dinner with your wife, which is unfair to her.
- You are planning a relaxing night at home after a very busy week. You are tired and just want to rest. Suddenly, your friend calls and asks you to come out. You don't want to, but your reply is, "Okay, I'll be there soon."

When you behave passively, you literally never get anything you want. Your life is easily swayed by someone else. You are simply going along so you can get along, which is totally against what an alpha male does. The passive male, in many ways, is worse than the aggressive male. At least the aggressive person is fighting for what they want, but their approach is incorrect. The passive person never fights for anything and remains in the passenger seat.

I am not saying you have to get into an argument or disagreement over every single thing. You can certainly pick your battle, but never sacrifice your principles or well-being for someone else. Stop living passively and begin living life as you should. I will go over some techniques shortly.

Being Passive-Aggressive:

Just like it sounds, this communication method is a combination of being passive and aggressive. Basically, you are letting your feelings be known, but in a very indirect way that is not clear. When people use this strategy, they are attempting to communicate their frustrations and dissatisfactions while avoiding any responsibility for them. This is probably the most aggravating style because it creates mass confusion for everyone involved. The individuals using it might think they are expressing themselves clearly, when they are actually not, while the individuals receiving the information are getting mixed messages. The following are some different examples of passive-aggressive styles of communication.

- Gossip: This is where you are expressing grievances about someone, or essentially talking smack, to individuals who are not the person you are upset with. Basically, you are criticizing someone and avoiding the consequences, because they don't know you are doing it.
- Sarcasm: This is a form of communication where you are taking a jab at someone in an indirect way, but playing if off as a joke. You will never take responsibility here because you always have an out.
- Getting out of doing something by acting incompetent, so they won't ask you to do it any longer.
- Instead of actually stating what you're angry about, you simply throw an attitude.

Passive-aggressive behavior might work in short spurts. When people are first getting to know us, they may be more accommodating with our grievances. After a while, though, this behavior gets on people's nerves and they stop caring what you have to say. The passive-aggressive person will be affected after a while too because they know they are not being honest in their approach, and this creates a lot of guilt.

Based on the results obtained from each communication style, there is no doubt that the assertive approach is the way to go. When you begin using this method to get your point across, you will be happier, and the people you speak to will be more appreciative. This is because you are clear, honest and responsive to them as well. To become an alpha male, your first step is to learn how to be assertive. I will show you how.

Communicating Like an Alpha

If you want to start acting like the alpha male you were meant to be, then it all starts with how you approach others with your communication style. This is how you either get your point across or fall by the wayside. Assertiveness does not just mean how you speak. It is how you behave overall. This includes body language, facial expressions, posture and tone of voice. Two people can literally say the same thing but send completely different messages due to these various factors.

Some men are naturally assertive, while others need to learn. In most cases, it is picked up through many environmental factors, like the other men in your life. This is great news because you can practice improving upon your poor communication strategies. If you are not used to being assertive, then it will take time, which is okay. Transforming yourself is not an easy process, especially when you become accustomed to acting a certain way. There are many barriers to assertive communication, and many of them come back to being afraid in some way.

- We are worried about getting judged for expressing our true feelings.

- We don't want to deal with drama or get guilt-tripped for not wanting to agree with someone.
- We feel more powerful than someone.
- We want to appear more confident than we are by being aggressive and hiding our insecurities.
- We don't want to take any responsibility for what we say or do.
- We are too anxious or nervous to express our feelings, especially if it's an unpopular opinion.
- It can take a lot of energy and effort to be assertive. It's often easier to just go with the crowd.

Being assertive can be even more difficult when the people around us are not used to it. They become confused and will often push back when we change our tune. Moments like these are critical because the actions we take next determine which direction we go. If we retreat after being challenged, then we lose the ground we have gained. If we stand our ground and push back, then people know we are serious. When we continue to stand our ground time after time, then we make some legitimate progress.

What Else Does Assertiveness Mean:

While we associate assertiveness mainly with how we speak or communicate, it goes beyond just this aspect. It also has to do with how we live our lives in the general sense. It is about holding true to our values and respecting ourselves enough to live our lives accordingly. This can mean a lot of things.

In the first place, assertive communication means that we keep our word. Anyone can speak like an assertive person, but if you do not follow through on what you say, we lose the trust we have gained with other people. Also, we undermine the trust within ourselves. If we do not honor our commitments, then we become known as unreliable and inconsistent. People lose respect for us because of this.

We must also stand behind the decisions we have made. Once we have done our research, listened to some sound advice and considered various different options, then the resulting decision we make must stand. We cannot just second-guess nonstop after coming to a conclusion, because we are effectively telling our brain that our instincts cannot be trusted. Unless there is something dire that comes to our attention, then we must stick to our decision and stand by the results.

Speaking of results, some things will not always go your way. No matter how sure you are about something, unexpected outcomes will occur. This is just a part of life and not an indictment on your decision-making skills. The key factor here is, you must stick with the decision you made, regardless of the results. This shows that you take responsibility for your life. There will always be variables that you cannot control, so don't dwell on those for long.

Being able to defend your beliefs is another indication of assertiveness. What often happens is that people have strong opinions about things, but immediately showcase their inability to defend them once they are challenged. Many individuals retreat and dismiss the views they held or they become overly aggressive in trying to defend them, which illustrates a deep uncertainty. The man who can defend himself calmly, clearly and respectfully is truly the one who can stand by his beliefs.

Finally, being assertive means that you welcome feedback. You understand that other people will view something differently and you might learn from them. People who do not welcome feedback are worried about getting challenged because they lack confidence.

As you can see, assertiveness goes alongside being an alpha male. If you do not start working on this trait, then all else will be lost.

How to Become Assertive:

I will now discuss specific strategies to help you become an assertive person. While this process will be simple to understand, it will not be easy. Gaining this essential skill takes time and effort. It needs to be built and developed through a lot of practice and repetition. I will tell you right now that if you are not willing to work on yourself daily, then you don't have enough desire to change for the better.

To avoid getting overwhelmed, start small and work your way up. Practice being assertive in more low-stakes situations, like letting the waiter or waitress know if you received the wrong meal. As you slowly gain confidence in your skills, then you can focus on more critical areas of your life, like career and relationships.

Remember that being assertive will feel very uncomfortable initially, even with smaller decisions. This is completely natural and you must not let it faze you. I cannot express how important it is not to back away from your true values and opinions. The following are some effective ideas you can start implementing right away to build up your assertiveness in life.

Make Imperfect Decisions:

What I mean is that if someone asks your opinion on something, express the first thing that comes to your mind. This may not be the perfect answer, but it will express your thoughts in real time. By doing this, you are also making an honest statement without any outside influence. Mind you, this does not have to be your final decision, but it gets your opinion out there quickly.

Ask for the Opposite of What You Are Being Offered:

This technique works well for situations that you do not care much about. However, it helps you build your ability to reject an offer you don't like, which opens up the path for further communication. As an example, if you are being seated at a restaurant, ask the person seating you politely for a different seat. You can say, "May we get another seat by the window, please." Be respectful, but firm. From here, if the individual says they don't have any available seating, you can ask them to double-check. It is your choice on how far you want to take this. Just don't create a scene or make the worker's life difficult.

I just want you to get used to asking for things you want, so do this often. Sometimes you'll get what you ask for and sometimes not. The important thing is that you tried and did not just accept things as they are.

Stop Apologizing When You Haven't Made a Mistake:

Do you find yourself saying "I'm sorry" before or after every sentence? We often automatically say this because we know other people are uncomfortable or we have a differing viewpoint. These instances are not calls for an apology. You apologize when you legitimately made a mistake, not because people don't approve of your behavior. Stop saying "sorry" all the time. One thing you can do is use the swear jar technique. Each time you say "sorry" for no reason, force yourself to put a nickel or other type of change in a jar. Empty it out once a week and try to reduce the amount you empty each time. Your goal is to eventually have no money in the jar, period.

Get Comfortable Saying "No":

This one will drive people nuts, because they hate being told "no." However, you must practice using this word and making it part of your vernacular. You will also be very uncomfortable when you start saying it, but stick to your guns and keep practicing. When you say it, do it with some authority. So, whenever someone asks you to do something you don't want, and it is unnecessary, then say "no" and move on.

Stop Saving the World:

You do not need to offer solutions to everyone else's problems. Sometimes, you have to allow people to solve problems on their own. Also, don't be so available to people where they think they can just interrupt your day and expect you to pay attention to them.

Start Voicing Your Opinions:

Begin with smaller issues in your life and start voicing your opinions on them when the opportunity arises.

As I mentioned before, becoming assertive does not happen overnight. It takes constant practice and once you've reached your goal, you must keep practicing to keep up your skills. The reason people stay at the top of their field is that they never stop training or learning. The same holds true for changing your attitude and mindset.

Picking Your Battles

I do not want to give the impression that you must challenge everything all the time and disagree with every person you come across. You must pick your battles, which means being selective about the problems, arguments and confrontations you get involved in.

If you are getting involved with every problem that comes your way, you will become exhausted and the important issues in your life will get ignored. I certainly want you to stand behind your beliefs and values, but I do not want you to always be at odds with people every chance you get. You might need to do this when you first start becoming assertive for practice, but you cannot sustain this way.

One of the main reasons being selective is important is that not everything will matter in the long run. Focus on the critical aspects of your life and prepare to defend those areas. For example, if you work for an office and they are ordering sushi for lunch, and you want pizza, then is it really a cause for getting worked up? Now, if you are expressing your wants and needs and always getting ignored, then it's time to speak up. Otherwise, let them have their sushi, or whatever, once in a while.

Remember that your time on Earth is limited and battles take up a significant amount of time. Even if you get what you desired, the time you spent arguing may not have been worth it. You could have focused on something more important. Imagine for a minute that you were busy arguing with a coworker about a parking space and missed an opportunity to explain to your boss why you deserve a raise.

Remember that when a lion is chasing down his prey, he does not stop for every animal that he passes along the way.

When you learn to become more assertive, I want you to focus on issues that are crucial for your life and happiness. The following are some tips on how to choose your battles carefully.

- Evaluate the problem carefully. If it is not really your problem or will have no issues for you in the long run, then it may be best to ignore them. For example, if an alpha male is walking down the street and gets called a name, he will probably just keep walking and not confront the guy. Now, if the guy gets in his face, then he becomes a real threat and the alpha will respond as needed.
- Is the investment in time worth the fight, even if you win? This is a cost-benefit analysis in the investing world. Not every benefit is worth the resources needed to achieve it.
- When you decide to pick a battle, ground yourself in high consciousness. Do not approach the fight with a state of anger. Remember the goal is to resolve the conflict, not destroy the other person.
- Work on achieving a win-win outcome. Remember that the goal of assertive communication is not to win, but to achieve a better result overall. This means that each involved party should benefit from the final decision. Aggressive people try to win. Assertive people try to make things better.
    - Open discussion, which is a trait of assertive communication, must be practiced to achieve a win-win scenario.
- Have an exit point. This means that you should be aware of how far you're willing to take a fight. Consider your resources and how long they will last. This includes time.

- Let go of unresolved problems. Despite our best efforts, some problems will not have a solution. Accept this fact and move on.

Remember the goal is to become an alpha male. This type of person knows when he needs to fight, and when he needs to stand back. In the end, the alpha male controls his life and circumstances, including what battles he gets involved in. Nothing can make him waver from this. So, stand up tall, defend your values, speak your mind and live with assertiveness. Once you do, then congratulations, because you are on your way to achieving alpha status.

Chapter 4:

The Laws of Attraction

"People are just as happy as they make up their minds to be."
- Abraham Lincoln

This powerful and relatable quote from President Abraham Lincoln showcases just how mighty the mind is. How we see the world, our thoughts, our happiness and, ultimately, our success relates back to our minds. People do not understand just how influential our mindset is in achieving the life we want. In order to become an alpha in your own life, the mindset shift is what needs to occur. You must realize now that your own mind is what ultimately determines whether you move forward or take a step back. Yes, there will be obstacles in your life, but to overcome them, you must believe that you can.

This last statement may sound a little cliché, but it is still true. Unfortunately, there is a misconception regarding the power of the mind. People have been led to believe that if you just sit there and think positive thoughts, then all of your problems will go away and you will be wealthy beyond your wildest imaginations. This is not what it means at all. The power of the mind truly comes into play by attracting the things we want, focusing on them then opening up a path for us to achieve our goals.

There is a major theory known as the Law of Attraction, which states that we have the ability to attract whatever we want in our lives if we give our full focus to it. The law implies that even if you think about something in a negative manner, you will still attract it because that is what your mind is focused on. For example, if you always think about poverty and how you want to avoid it, you will still experience poverty in your life, because that is what you are constantly thinking about. If you want to avoid poverty, then don't even let it cross your mind and give all of your attention to gaining success and wealth.

As we live our lives, whether knowingly or unknowingly, every moment of our existence consists of us walking around like magnets. The thoughts and emotions we put out there, ultimately attract the same ones back. If we are sad, the universe picks up on these emotional vibes and sends them to us. As a result, we end up living in perpetual sadness and, no matter what good things happen, we remain sad because we choose to be.

Even if you're not aware of the Law of Attraction, you are still creating your reality. For this reason, we must understand the importance of the law from all facets and recognize how it affects our world. Even if we ignore the Law of Attraction, it will definitely not ignore us. Once you understand the theory, then you can purposefully start changing your thoughts and feelings and, in turn, your reality.

The Law of Attraction is not some sort of complicated quantum physics formula. It really is as simple as it sounds -- at least in the practical sense. What you think about in life is what you ultimately attract. The key is that you must be aware of the tone of your thoughts at all times.

Law of Attraction History

Before I go any further with concepts, it's important to revisit the history behind the Law of Attraction to understand its full weight. While the actual phrase did not gain steam until modern times, the actual principles behinds have been utilized throughout the course of history. Many of the world's religions, like Buddhism, Hinduism, Christianity and Islam, incorporate many of the same ideas in their teachings.

The earliest origins of the Law of Attraction are thought to date back to the times of the immortal Buddha. He wanted to spread the belief that you will ultimately become what you speak. This idea is the foundation for this powerful law. Buddha wanted people to realize how powerful their own thoughts were and how they should not be underestimated. His teachings were accepted by many of his followers.

> *"All that we are is a result of what we have thought."*
> \- Buddha

While the teachings of Buddha highlighted this concept, it is believed that humanity has always held some level of awareness of it. Basically, people have always understood, to some degree, that their mind attracts what it thinks about. For example, some of the interpretations of Jesus' teachings can be to create limitless power.

During the 19th century, a spiritually gifted author, Helena Blavatsky, enhanced the concept of our thoughts creating our reality during the New Thought Movement. In her 1888 book, *The Secret Doctrine,* her ideas were heavily related to the modern-day Law of Attraction. In particular, she contended that our thoughts about ourselves are what define who we are and what we're capable of.

> *"The universe is guided from within outwards."*
> \- Helena Blavatsky

Many other important figures during the 19th and 20th centuries contributed to the idea of the Law of Attraction. In 1937, Napoleon Hill wrote the famous book, *Think and Grow Rich,* which heavily promoted the techniques of this law. He aimed to show that we can all overcome challenges and use manifestation tools to create a happy and fulfilling life. Mr. Hill used many of his own experiences and struggles to make a point. His book became a worldwide sensation and is still referenced until today in many different settings, like business and relationships.

"Whatever the mind can conceive and believe, it can achieve."
- Napoleon Hill

Other influential figures during the 20th century, like Esther Hicks and Louise Hay, also played a role in the growth of the Law of Attraction. Hicks discusses the Law and its importance in her collection of books called, *The Teachings of Abraham*. Meanwhile, Hay popularized the idea of using affirmations.

In the 21st century, the Law of attraction went from a niche interest to gaining worldwide fame when Rhonda Byrne's wrote her book, *The Secret*. She also had an associated film that followed shortly after. *The Secret* presents many teachings and views of a wide array of practitioners of the Law, including authors, entertainers, philosophers and scientists. The film also contains pearls of wisdom from people like Joe Vitale and Jack Canfield. It also stresses the importance of goal setting, eliminating negative energy and learning new ways to think.

The Law of Attraction has become even more popular since *The Secret* came out because many celebrities have credited its teachings with their own success. Actor Will Smith credits the book and film for many positive experiences in his own life. The Law of Attraction has become a popular mainstream idea, but it's a concept that has been around for centuries.

The teachings have a vast history, which shows that they are not just some new-age fad. They have been adopted by many cultures of the world throughout time.

The Evidence Behind the Law of Attraction

Humans have a certain relationship to the universe. Some people believe they feel like they are not in control of their lives as the universe completely decides what will happen to them. The goal of following the Law of Attraction is to realize that they happen to the universe. People put out their thoughts and feelings for the universe to listen to and they receive the same level of thoughts and feelings in return. Once you start shifting your mindset to understand this concept, then good things will start happening to you. You will attract a better life.

It's Science, Not Fantasy:

Many people are not convinced by the Law of Attraction. They see it as some magic spell that self-help gurus try to put them under. I admit that the Law is not fully understood at this time. It can be hard to understand how it is scientific in nature, mainly because it is dealing with intangible concepts, like thoughts and feelings. With something like the law of gravity, we can see how it works by the fact that we are not all floating away, even though there's nothing visible on top of us. Also, if we throw something into the air, like a ball, it will come right back down. We don't have the same visuals with the Law of Attraction.

Of course, advances in science and technology now allow us to immediately experience the effects of our thoughts. These new advances give us the visual ball moment that we need. In this section, I will go over some scientific experiments that prove the Law of Attraction to be factual.

The Meditation Experiment:

In the summer of 1993 in Washington D.C., about 4,000 people volunteered to meditate on peace and love to help reduce the crime rate of the city, which was rampant at the time. The experiment was approached without any bias and with a goal to lower violent crime by 20 per cent. During the same month, the crime rate dropped by 18 percent. As the positive thoughts swarmed through the city, so did the people's mindsets.

The Youth Experiment:

In 1979, a study showed that thinking you are physically younger actually makes you younger. During the experiment, several men between the ages of 70 to 80 were split into two separate groups. One group was asked to fondly remember things about their youth, while the second group actually pretended to be young by surrounding themselves with music, activities and TV shows from their youths.

When the experiment was completed, the group that imagined they were younger actually became younger, not just mentally, but physically too. They felt younger, had lower blood pressure, had more energy and less pain from arthritis. Even their hearing and eyesight improved. Physical aging was actually reversed because of how these men viewed themselves.

The Water Experiment:

Japanese Scientist, Dr. Masaru Emoto, conducted one of the most famous experiments of all time to show the power of our thoughts. Using some water crystals as his subjects, he photographed them while projecting thoughts of either love and peace or hate and fear at them. Sometimes the intentions were spoken out loud, while other times, they were just thought inside of his head.

In the end, the crystals that were inundated by positive emotions like love and peace came out as perfectly beautiful and symmetrical. On the other hand, negative emotions resulted in disproportionate and broken water crystals. These outcomes further prove how our mental state impacts the physical world we live in.

Order Emerges from Chaos in the Universe, Nature, and Daily Life:

While our environment is filled with chaos, there are specific circumstances where complete order always emerges, showing true synchronicity in the universe, nature and ourselves. For example, the moon's rotation is synced with Earth, so that we always see the same face of the moon. Also, the human brain can fire off neurons in a specific frequency called neuronal synchrony. Finally, free-floating photons can be concentrated and focused to create lasers. The synchronicity shown in these examples illustrates that order can occur in our minds if we focus our attention on it.

These various experiments and observations during modern times illustrate the power of our minds and the effectiveness of the Law of Attraction. These were all independent studies that pointed to similar outcomes in the end. This points to the fact that the law is not just a magical theory, but has significant scientific backing.

In the end, approaching life with a positive attitude allows for better outcomes anyway. It is easier to keep our minds open and come up with solutions more effectively when we keep our thoughts productive and useful. Think about the obstacles you have faced in your own life and assess whether it was easier to overcome with a positive or negative attitude.

Where can the Law of Attraction Help You?

With the way the Law of Attraction works, it is not selective and can benefit you in every area of your life. Many individuals have a tendency to believe in themselves in one area, but completely neglect different aspects of your life. To use the theories we have discussed properly, you must have positive thoughts all around and not ignore any part of your life. This law can be beneficial for your wealth, relationships, health, happiness and other crucial areas in your life.

Attract More Money:

Gaining financial abundance is the number-one reason people become interested in the Law of Attraction. Money can be hard to come by and people get tired of working hard and only receiving a small paycheck every week. When they hear that they can attract more money simply by changing their thoughts, it becomes very appealing to them. It's no wonder then, that gaining wealth is a huge motivational factor for incorporating these powerful theories into their lives.

Once you learn the techniques involved, then you will start seeing immediate changes. You may not gain extreme wealth overnight, but small transitions will start to occur, which will guide you towards the direction of financial abundance. People begin to get unexpected checks, like those from loved ones. In addition, investments start to improve and new job opportunities come up. The money will not magically appear, but it will feel like it does on occasion.

Manifest Love and Better Relationships:

Finding true love and meaningful relationships is the next most popular reason people seek out the Law of Attraction. People long for deep connections, like those found in lifelong partners. Unfortunately, it can seem like an elusive game that cannot be won, no matter how hard it is played. It is a wonder why some people find love quickly, while others never experience it throughout their lives.

The Law of Attraction means working on yourself and your desires, so it inherently makes you a more attractive person with a clear vision of your goals. This allure becomes appealing to other people, including your potential partner. Once you learn the techniques of the Law of attraction, you will have a great tool at your disposal for finding love.

Better Health:

Our health is often an ignored aspect of our lives, even though it is the most important. Without our health, we will have nothing left. It is important to realize that the Law of Attraction can be used to manifest better physical and mental outcomes. Since our thoughts affect our physical reality, you might be attracting poor health without even realizing it. Thinking positively about your health can go a long way in improving it.

Spiritual Awakening:

The Law of attraction will connect you with higher spiritual planes of existence. You will begin to see beyond the physical world and a whole new sphere you never knew existed will open up to you, which will be brimming with new opportunities. You will begin to understand how much the universe has to offer in terms of abundance. Soon, you will learn that you are connected to everything around you and everything is connected to you in a harmonious relationship.

You Will Have More Fun:

The opportunities that come from the Law of Attraction are only limited by your imagination and the laws of physics. I don't want you to start thinking you're invincible here. The principles of this law can be used in many ways to attract more happiness and good karma into your lives. Therefore, you can create a reality that is more fun for you.

Think about the areas in your life that you have either ignored or thought negatively about. Have you been using phrases like, "I wish I wasn't overweight," "Why am I struggling financially" or "Why do people disrespect me all the time"? Well, these statements are negative, and even though you don't enjoy these things about your life, you are still inadvertently attracting them by keeping them in your mind. The Law of Attraction is very strict about what your mind needs to be focused on. To manifest a positive life, you must focus on positive things.

Instead of wondering why you're overweight, start picturing yourself skinny. Instead of thinking how lonely you are, start imagining your perfect partner. What you put inside your mind, is what you bring to you, despite what direction you may think about it.

How to use the Law of Attraction

Now that you know the foundations of the Law of Attraction and what it can manifest, it is time to start using the strategies to gain the life you want. There are several steps in the process that you must learn, understand and perform, in order to start transforming your dreams into your reality. Not only will I mention the steps, but also how to do them right.

Before we actually begin, there are a few things you must understand. First, really think about the areas of your life you want to focus on and start there. For example, if money is not important to you or you're happy with your current status, then don't pay much mind to this area. Think about where your life is now and where you want it to be. This is very personal to you. Some individuals want a house on the beach, some want a condo in a big metro area while others want an isolated cabin in the woods.

A major foundation in the Law of Attraction is to believe that it works. If you are doubtful, then you will not be fully committed. This may seem like an excuse, but it's true. If you want the techniques to be effective, then you must believe 100 percent in their power.

To build your confidence in its effectiveness, try the techniques out on smaller things first. Test it out and become comfortable with the strategies. Once you master them on a minor scale, then you can build it up from there. Small things include believing that you'll find a parking space quickly, money will turn up to afford groceries or you will reconnect with an old friend. Once these things begin to unfold in your life, then you will gain confidence in the process.

The law of Attraction is a concept that many great leaders and influential people use around the world. Whether you believe in it or not, it is working to build up your reality. As you've come to understand the basics of this law, you can now pay attention to your thoughts and make sure they reflect what you want out of life. It's worth a try, even if you still find it far-fetched. Now that you've reached this point, it's time to focus on the techniques.

Decide What You Want:

This is the first and most crucial step in the whole process. If you do not make this decision properly, then the whole foundation will crumble. Don't rush. Take all the time you need because the decisions you make here will determine the areas of your life that will get the most attention and, therefore, the greatest results.

Think about how you want to feel. Also, what areas of your life are you not happy with at all? For this step, you can write down what you don't like about your life to get an idea of what you want. After this, start changing your focus. Ask yourself this important question: If money was not a factor, where would you be living, where would you be working, and what would you be doing?

- Remember to think about what you actually want, and not what you think you should have, based on society's expectations.
- You don't have to come up with reasons for your decision. Just come up with what you want. For example, just wanting a bigger house on the beach is good enough without creating a rationale.
- The excitement you feel when you make a decision should indicate how important it is in your life.

"You are a living magnet. What you attract into your life is in harmony with your dominant thoughts."

- Brian Tracy

Positive emotions that result from a decision speed up the manifestation.

Visualize the Decision:

Visualization is a very powerful tool to help you foresee what you want. This can be a picture in your mind, a drawing or an actual photograph. Creating something that gives you a visual representation of your dreams is essential. Using your mind to see a future outcome means you are inviting that thing into your life.

To do this properly, sit in bed or wherever you sleep every night and picture the end result of your manifestation. For example, you can envision a house, a particular travel destination, a number that represents money or a perfect mate. Once again, you can use a physical picture of some sort if that helps. Just make sure you look at it frequently.

Performing this before going to sleep saves the image into your subconscious mind, so make sure the visual is as clear as possible. As your subconscious mind starts filling up with your desired images, your reality will begin shifting.

Don't try to figure out how your vision is going to come into your life. For now, just imagine it and let it get ingrained in your mind. Let yourself go with the fantasy and really try to feel the emotions that come with it. How would you feel if the visual became a reality? Once again, these emotions will be a powerful tool.

Believe Your Dream is on the Way

Many people do not believe something will happen until it actually does. For the Law of Attraction to work, you must believe that your dream is coming, even before you see it. Remember that the goal is to attract things with our thoughts. If you don't believe that something is coming, then you are not pulling it in. The universe will not know that you want it.

Once you believe that what you're waiting for is coming, then the universe will start aligning things accordingly to bring it to you. Tell yourself that it's yours already, and it will be on its way. Some people use the trick of pretending they already have whatever they want by physically putting it in their hands. For example, if someone wants wealth, they will write themselves a check for a certain amount and just hold onto it. If someone wants a house, they will create a congratulatory letter and keep it on their desk. These steps may seem silly, but they will keep your attention on the prize.

At this point, you have made the decision, visualized it and put your full belief in it. The universe now understands what you want and will make it happen. Let's just be clear about something. If your focus is on financial abundance, $1 million is not going to fall on top of you from the sky. That's not how the universe works. What will happen is that more avenues will open up to you so that you can make financial abundance a reality. For example, new job opportunities may arise, you may come up with a great business idea out of nowhere or one of your investments may take off. We don't know exactly how the universe works, we just know that it will work in your favor if you allow it to.

One more word of advice: Once you tell the universe your dreams, pay attention to the answers it gives you. If you don't, then you will miss out on a lot of opportunities.

Law of Attraction Meditation

Sometimes, we become so inundated with life, that we are unclear about what we actually want. We cannot make any positive decisions, because our mind becomes clouded. In these moments, it may be the right moment to step back from the sources of frustration and clear your mind.

The time and space we give ourselves to be alone help us figure out who we are and what's important to us. We have a real opportunity to calm our souls. Once we do this, then we can make better decisions. If you have no meditation experience, then here are a few steps to get you started.

- Find a quiet area with no distractions. Leave your phone in another room, if you can. Close your eyes and focus on slowing down your breathing.
- Repeat a word that is uplifting for you.
- Move into a state of quietness.
- Keep your mind and thoughts centered, do not allow them to drift. Do not start thinking about your job or the bills you have to pay.
- Sit in this position for at least a couple of minutes.
- Imagine yourself surrounded by a beam of light.

The great news is that there are plenty of books on meditation. Also, there are plenty of practitioners that you can learn from.

You probably noticed that the Law of Attraction is not complicated when you put it into practice. It is a simple technique to understand with very fundamental steps. The key is repetition and commitment. You must invest time and belief in these practices and perform them on a daily basis. The more you tell the universe what you want, the more likely you are to get it.

Why Should Alpha Males Follow This?

It may seem like we took a slight deviation from the rest of the book, but we actually didn't. A large aspect of becoming an alpha male is the mindset you carry. Following the Law of Attraction forces you to think positively about your life and potential goals. This leads to great success. As an alpha male, your goal will be to succeed in every area of your life, and getting help from the universe will make it happen for you.

Men who do not believe in the Law of Attraction also don't believe they can have abundance in life. They have no confidence or self-worth, which means they are either beta or omega males. Alpha males, whether they know what the Law of Attraction is or not, incorporate its practices into their everyday routine. They become better men because of it.

Remember to dream big. Since you are putting positive vibes out into the universe anyway, put out the grandest ones you can think of based on what your goals are. Alpha males do not think small. They think about how much success they can achieve and figure out a way to get it.

The Law of Attraction has been proven time and again. It has been around for centuries and continues to grow in popularity. Almost any good business, self-help seminar, life coach or adviser picks out aspects of this theory for their own practices. If other people have found success from it, then so can you.

Chapter 5:

Reclaim Your Masculinity

Imagine for a moment that a big, aggressive-looking man walks into a store. He has an angry look on his face as he looks around. He walks through the aisles and gathers whatever supplies he needs then stands in line, which is quite long. After about a minute, he audibly says, "Screw this," then cuts in line while throwing his money on the counter. He then shoves the door violently open and walks out.

The other customers are perplexed at what just happened. They see a man like this and automatically start thinking that he's a product of toxic masculinity or he's letting out his male aggression. The reason so many people may start thinking this way is because of what they've been force-fed about manhood and being a male, in general. As a result, when many in the public hear phrases or words like, "alpha male," or "masculinity," they get a visceral reaction. Even several men have started shielding themselves from these phrases to the point they are ashamed of being men.

Many males are confused as to how they should act, then develop personalities based on what they think society believes a man should be. The problem is society's opinions on the matter are based largely on misrepresentations. Basically, they have characterization and image of a man that is aggressive, mean, uncaring and a total bully. They start feeling that all men are like this and get a sour opinion about all males, as a whole.

Over time, this has resulted in mass confusion. Any time a man is confident and straightforward, or stands up for himself, he is seen as overly aggressive. Men are now expected to act in a diminutive fashion and just be seen, but not heard. What society, and men, need to realize is that masculinity is not inherently negative. It is not about being angry, aggressive, domineering, controlling or arrogant. This is something I have touched on earlier in this book, but really want to drive home now. There are so many falsehoods out there and I will dispel them right here and right now. After completing this chapter, you will be proud to be a man that women admire as a real man.

Masculinity Should Not be Avoided

There have been many instances in recent times of extreme violent acts being perpetrated on society. These acts include mass shootings, gang fights, assaults on the most vulnerable populations, like the elderly and even police brutality. These many instances are exclusive to one another, but they have some commonality, and that is that most of them are done by men. At least, the ones that make the headlines do. I bet most of us would be hard-pressed to think of a day when we were watching the news and everything remained peaceful. Violence seems to have taken over our streets and no end in sight is currently visible.

The more the public sees these horrific images with faces of men at the forefront, the more they are inclined to view males as violent, aggressive and cruel individuals who are bad for society. I admit many men out there do not help the cause with their brash and chauvinistic behavior. Some cultures even encourage male domination and do not allow women to even have a voice. As a whole, men do not have a positive image out there.

What people don't realize is that the profiles showcased of men after committing horrible acts, whether they are school shootings, or otherwise, are not understood in their entirety. What I mean is that these men are depressed, lonely, diminutive and scared. They are the type of men who feel powerless and oppressed, and therefore, they take it out on people to gain some of their power back. These are not real men with masculine qualities. So, one can say that males commit violent crimes because they have not been allowed to be men. At least not real men.

Real men express themselves regularly. They are kind, compassionate and loving, but will be assertive, firm, strong and straightforward when they need to be. Real men do not hide their emotions, which is kind of confusing because that's what many men are expected to do. They will simply showcase them in a brave and stoic manner. One thing for sure is, that you will not be confused about how a true man feels. He will have no problem telling you he is pissed off. This may be off-putting or hurtful in the moment, but at least they are not holding everything in until they eventually explode and commit the heinous acts that make the news. I am not trying to make excuses here, but the men who do lose it and create newsworthy moments are those who have been pushed to the edge. Their only way out, as they see it, is to lash out at others.

The media have caused many to believe that *all* males act like these men and they ruin the world for everybody. However, some of the greatest men in history were actually quite masculine. Men like Dr. Martin Luther King, Jr., Mahatma Gandhi, Franklin D. Roosevelt, Nelson Mandela and Abraham Lincoln changed the world in their own unique ways because they were brave enough to do so. These were masculine men, who were not perfect but displayed positive qualities of courage, strength, love and compassion. Yes, they were a product of their times, which created many of their faults, but overall, they were good men.

When was the last time you heard about a meek and meager man making history in a positive way? These men usually get lost in the shuffle, which contributes to their depression and even anger. I use the term depression here loosely because it is a medical term and must be diagnosed officially. Nonetheless, powerless men are not known for great things and often don't get any attention until they do something outrageous. For some reason, people put their acts of atrocity at the forefront of their minds and forget about the actions of good men.

The few weak men in our world who rise above and become alpha males can eventually do great things. Otherwise, they are forgotten commodities. I want you to become one of the men who rise above and change themselves. I want you to realize that hiding from masculinity is taking you on a destructive path. If you continue down this route, you may or may not harm someone else, but you will definitely hurt yourself. The weak beta or omega males who don't commit violent acts against others often engage in other self-destructive behaviors.

What is Masculinity:

With all of the various stereotypes that exist out there related to manhood, it is difficult to pinpoint what masculinity is supposed to look like. Is it the football player, the high-powered CEO, the MMA fighter, the work-a-holic or the stay-at-home dad? Well, it can be all of these and more. Masculinity is not defined by what a man does, but by who he is. I mentioned earlier in the book about how stereotypical roles often get confused for classic manhood. These roles actually do not relate to being a man, per se. This means that the gay hairdresser with purple hair who gets pedicures might actually be more masculine than the buff construction worker with a beard and dirty hands.

Masculinity goes much deeper than this. It's what exists deep within a man's soul. For example, a man is not masculine because he works at a construction site, but because he is willing to work night and day in dangerous settings and inclement weather to take care of his family. The hairdresser is masculine because he is not afraid to express himself and is doing the job he wants, despite what others may think of him. Plus, he is working hard to make a living, so he has purpose in life.

At its core, masculinity means having certainty in action. It is not getting bound by the opinions of other people and doing the tasks needed to live the life you want. You don't have to be perfect to be masculine, but you need to have some certainty about who you are and what your future looks like.

How to Promote Masculinity:

Well, the main thing we need to do, which will not be easy, is to stop indoctrinating the world against real men. The world of academia needs to stop diminishing the value men bring to the table. Teachers need to stop telling boys to stop doing natural boy things, like playing in the dirt, imagining they're superheroes or roughhousing. Remember, roughhousing is not the same as fighting. It is boys having fun and developing their brains by doing so.

There have been many commercials, TV shows, and movies since the 1990s that also show men in a negative light. They are either bumbling buffoons or overly aggressive jerks. More media that shows real men in a positive light is essential. This will take time and the involvement of many people. There is no easy way to do this. Honestly, the breakdown of men has occurred over many decades, and it may take that amount of time to fix. Unfortunately, I don't know the answer.

The best way I can assist is to help change one man at a time. I urge all of you men out there to act like real men and show the rest of the world that masculinity is not the enemy. Masculinity, in its true form, is necessary to make the world run. No, I am not saying that men are more important than women. Both are equally essential in creating a more positive world. Each sex brings their own unique strengths to the table which needs to be valued and recognized. The remainder of this chapter will discuss various techniques to help build your masculinity in a productive fashion. After going through all of these, you will be the type of man we all need and will wear it as a badge of honor.

Be a Man, Not a Jerk

Now that we have established what being a man means, it's time to take positive steps forward. Manhood still needs to be celebrated in society and we can all do our parts by becoming the best men we can be. To begin the process in the right direction, you need to stop and ask yourself one important question: What action steps can I take right now to be more certain about my life and circumstances?

Stop worrying about what other people think or say. They are not you and should not have control over your decisions. Also, start letting go of your past. It cannot be changed and, therefore, should not matter in your present situation. When you have the answer to the above question, then it's time to start taking action. By that, I mean massive action to create great change in your life. Don't get me wrong, small progress is still progress, but I want you to start making as many changes as you can.

Masculine people take action to find certainty. They are actively creating their future, rather than letting their future create them. It really is this simple to get started. To break it down further, consider the following questions.

- What situation is causing you the most uncertainty in life?
- What steps can you come up with that will help you get past this uncertainty?
- What is stopping you? Why have you not taken action yet?

Answer these questions and start acting, then you are on your way to becoming masculine. Now, I want to warn you about something. There will come a time when people test you. These people will cause you some uncertainty about your life. They will piss you off royally and you will want to retaliate in a negative way. This does not mean yelling at them or punching them in the face to solve the problem. While this is an action step that can eliminate some uncertainty, it just makes you a jerk in the end. Real men do not fight unless it is absolutely necessary. Someone being an idiot to you is not a cause for violence, no matter how good it might make you feel later. The only time I promote violence is if you are using it to defend yourself or someone else. Even then, use just enough to get you out of the situation.

In a situation where you feel angry enough to hurt someone, you will still know on the conscious level that it is wrong. A good way to overcome this feeling to go through the process of taking ownership.

As a man and an adult, there are certain things that you contributed to a situation to make it like it is. It is important to recognize what these are, so you can fix them immediately. Taking ownership will allow you to understand that your actions have consequences, which includes getting you into situations you don't want to be in. In the example above, you can think about things you might have done to make the people target you. Did you say or do something that caused them to behave in that manner? If so, then you can admit it, apologize and move on. Focus on what you can do to prevent similar issues in the future then follow the steps to make it happen.

Then there's the other side. This is what you can't control, which are the actions of other people. Unfortunately, other people do contribute to your pain and suffering, whether it is with words or actions. Taking ownership does not mean you are fully to blame for a bad situation; it means controlling your own behavior and ignoring that of others. Other people are more vested in their happiness than yours. This is not a bad thing, just a reality. Therefore, it is a waste of time trying to figure them out. Move on and only deal with them if you have no choice.

Why Taking Ownership is Beneficial:

This realization removes the blame towards outward circumstances and lets us focus on ourselves. We pay attention to what we can control and nothing else. This provides two distinct benefits:

- You will feel less angry because ownership gives you a path to solving life's challenges. When you focus on your contributions, then you set up a plan to eliminate issues from your life.
- Your rage will not be directed towards someone else. Instead, you will be frustrated with yourself and will do your best to not have these feelings again.

This might sound unfair, but trust me. When you start taking ownership, you will be happier and more productive. Your life will start to progress as it should and what others are doing will no longer impact you.

Here is an example of a situation where you can take ownership, which is very common. You are having a hard time paying your bills. You are in debt and can barely hold your head above water. In this situation, it will be easy to blame others. For instance, someone else might have gotten a promotion over you, maybe your boss doesn't value you, the electrical company is charging more, your car insurance rates went up and your friends stole from you. All of these things suck; there's no doubt about that. However, if you focus on them, you will get nowhere. Instead, look inside and determine what changes you can make. Can you ask for a raise? Is it possible to work extra hours at your job for additional income? Do you have the ability to get a second job? Are there any expenses in your life you can cut out? Have you learned not to let your friends take advantage of you? When you begin taking ownership, you start coming up with real solutions.

How to Take Ownership:

There really isn't a lot to say here. Taking ownership is not something complicated that you have to study. You simply have to make it a regular part of your life. Always remember the question: How or what did I contribute to creating frustration and annoyance in my life? Any time you feel this way, step back and ask this question. Do it often enough, and you will slowly start to solve all of your problems. Congratulations! You are on the way to becoming more masculine.

> *"You must own everything in your world. No one else is to blame."*
>
> - Jocko Willink

Creating Your Masculine Edge

Many men in our world today do not feel like they are men. They lack direction, passion, fire and a winning spirit. All of these are needed to win in life, while the absence of these factors explains why so many men are not winners. They are placed on the backburners in their own lives and are given zero amount of respect. They get walked all over, ignored and chastised constantly. The problem continues to grow as men become weaker and weaker. It is time to change this phenomenon by rekindling the masculine edge.

The masculine edge is the natural energy that a man carries to get his work done and live his ultimate life. A man who carries this edge is not one to be trifled with. Though he will not be aggressive towards someone for no reason, he will not hesitate to put someone down who messes with him. He has no false bravado. He does not walk around showing how tough he is. However, when people look at him, they know he is somebody.

When you stand face-to-face with a man with the masculine edge, he will have a calmness about him. However, you will know he can switch almost instantly. It is like staring at a caged lion. When you are in his presence, you will know he is the man you desire to be. Guess what? You can become him. I will show you how.

Benefits of the Masculine Edge:

There are many benefits to having the masculine edge, and really, it relates to being an alpha male, in general.

- Deeper and more fulfilling relationships. This includes romantic relationships.
- More consistent energy and zest for life.
- More passion for your work, even if you don't necessarily like your job.

- Greater amount of respect from others, mainly because you command it.
- More courage and confidence to get through the day.
- More honest and deep conversations.
- More fulfilling sex life.
- A better life, in general, with more fun and excitement.

Are these reasons appealing enough for you to continue? I hope so.

Steps to Develop Your Masculine Edge:

Like most of the concepts in this book, developing the masculine edge is a simple process, but it will take time, effort and consistency. The following are the most effective steps to creating your new manhood.

Presence:

Having a masculine edge requires you to have a presence. This means you have the ability to give your full attention without getting distracted. Once you develop this ability, then you will be the embodiment of pure consciousness. The key here is to not let external sources tap into your internal energy.

For you to become present, you must start setting appropriate boundaries. Learn to say "no" without any explanation. Anything you don't want to invest your energy in, don't be a part of it. Spend time around people who uplift you and get rid of energy vampires. You will now be able to give your energy and focus on things that matter in your life.

When with other people, always be observant and make good eye contact. Do not use your eyes to intimidate, but simply observe and react. Some other techniques you can use to increase your ability to be present, include:
- Doing yoga or mindful meditation.

- Going for walks in nature without distractions, such as technology.
- Declutter and reorganize your physical environment.
- Take time to slow down and enjoy your surroundings. You don't have to be busy all the time.

Increasing Passion and Intensity:

Having no passion or intensity in life is a surefire reason to lack a masculine edge. You need to find out what you're passionate about. What do you yearn for? What do you have that you would give your life to protect? Ask yourself these questions because you need to have something in your life that stokes your fire.

Cultivate a Future Focus:

To be masculine, you must have a sense of direction. You must understand where your life is headed and not just wander aimlessly. This does not mean that you have a strict career and follow an exact routine every day. It simply means you are living life with purpose towards something.

If you have a love interest in mind, then go directly towards them. Find a career that aligns with your values and beliefs and give it everything you have. If your goal is to create a healthier body, then go for it and make it happen.

Determine exactly what you want in life and set up ways to get it done. Don't let anything stand in your way. If there are things you need to eliminate in your life to reach your goals, then do it. This includes people. Not everyone deserves a place in your life, no matter who they are or how long you have known them.

Speak Your Truth:

Speak your truth as you see it, regardless of if people agree with you or not. This means not lying, not stretching things and not speaking out of both sides of your mouth. Be straightforward and tell the whole truth.

The truth can hurt, but you need to get into the habit of speaking it regularly. Once you do, you will feel better about yourself and have a more fulfilling life.

Put Your Needs Ahead of Others:

Putting other people's needs ahead of yourself means that you care about the perception others have of you. You are giving away all of your power when you do this. Stop seeking the approval of others and begin seeking it within yourself. When you look at yourself in the mirror, you must be proud of what you see, despite what others think.

If you try to please everyone, then you will please no one. People are never satisfied with what you give them. You must swing the pendulum to the other side and practice healthy selfishness. This means putting your needs first, then you can better help someone else. If your cup is empty, then you cannot fill anyone else's.

Become Comfortable With Social Tension:

People do not like to face tension and this is a common problem with many "nice guys." They never want to rock the boat or cause disagreements. To gain any type of success in life, you need to be willing to create social tension. This means walking up to the girl you like, asking your boss for a raise and telling your neighbor that his garbage is coming into your yard. The more comfortable you get with uncomfortable conversations, the more of a masculine edge you will cultivate.

Start having challenging conversations with people on a small scale. This can mean disagreeing on lunch, wearing a blue tie when your partner wants a black-tie or deciding what movie you want to see, even if others in your group don't like it. From here, move onto tougher situations like confronting a friend or coworker, asking a girl out on a date, or going into your boss' office to air your grievances. Of course, do all of this respectfully. I am not telling you to pick fights, but just get used to disagreeing with people. As you make yourself uncomfortable, your confidence will grow.

Be Okay With Being Emotional:

Big boys don't cry! That's probably a phrase you have heard throughout your life. Men aren't supposed to cry or show emotion unless they are those of anger, happiness or pride. Well, I am here to give you permission to express all of your emotions. Connect with your heart and gut to determine what emotions you are feeling and don't be afraid to show them. This is how you allow full happiness into your life. You have to let yourself feel all of your emotions, in order to fully feel any of them.

I admit that you have to keep yourself together in certain situations and cannot just break down. When you have the opportunities to do so, then let yourself feel rage, sadness, joy or whatever else is going through your mind.

Spend Time With Male Friends:

Are guys' nights out still a thing? I hope so because they are necessary to cultivate a masculine edge. Spending time with other men can be a magical moment for us with some great results. We often get called out legitimately by men we respect, which ignites a fire under us. We also feel a sense of brotherhood. Finally, we may rekindle a past relationship that has gone south. Time spent with male friends can be anything, like playing poker, going to a sporting event, having a BBQ or going to the gym. Whatever it may be, spend dedicated time during the week with only men and see how this makes you feel. As a caveat, remember to spend time with men you genuinely enjoy being around. Don't have to seek out the company of men who are jerks.

Practice Manly Hobbies:

Now, I am not saying that men cannot be interested in hobbies that are considered more feminine, like sewing or cooking, but many activities have a way of getting you in touch with your natural strengths. Many hobbies include weight lifting, hiking, bungee jumping, martial arts or competitive sports.

Take Care of Your Body:

Taking care of yourself is essential to performing any activity in your life. This means you must exercise, eat right, drink plenty of water, sleep well at night and avoid self-destructive behavior. Doing all of these will give you physical energy, boost your mood, sharpen your mind and allow you to tackle essential tasks.

Remember That Life is Limited:

While people are living their lives much longer on average, we still have no idea when our last day will be. Be aware of your mortality and know that you will die someday. Use this knowledge to motivate yourself. This will give your life meaning. Some people are crippled by this thought because they fear death. I want you to be inspired by it and live your life to the fullest.

Ask your this: "What would I be doing if I knew I would die tomorrow?" Whatever that is, figure out a way to do it (within reason, of course).

Perform these simple steps and strategies every day of your life. You will begin noticing massive changes in your life. Start killing off that "nice guy" you have been living as and become that real man you were meant to be.

How to Appear Masculine

The information we have covered in this book so far has been geared more towards feeling more masculine on the inside. Another important factor is to look masculine on the outside. The first impression people get of you is external, so it's good to give off the best image you can. You will hold more authority this way. Appearing masculine does not mean you have to be the tallest, biggest, or strongest man in the room. It does not mean you must have the best hair or expensive clothes. However, when people look at you, they should see the image of a real man. The following are some things to consider for appearing masculine on the outside.

Posture:

How you carry yourself will communicate to others about how you feel. If you are walking with a slouch, then people will see you as having no confidence. When you stand up straight, with your shoulders back, your chest out and your head held high, you look more masculine. As you do this, keep a relaxed look as well. Make it seem natural and do not exaggerate the posture. Standing there looking tense or wooden will not make you look sure of yourself.

Make Good Eye Contact:

You don't have to glare or keep looking at the same spot the whole time. A person just needs to know they have your full attention when talking to you. One thing you can do is focus on one eye, then switch to the other eye after a few minutes, then look at the mouth. This way you are rotating where you look but still maintaining eye contact.

Be Relaxed:

A masculine man will always appear at ease. That shows that they are comfortable in any situation. Take deep breaths throughout the day, especially when you feel your anxiety levels going up. Learn about other mindfulness techniques too, such as yoga, tai chi or meditation.

Dress Well:

A masculine man exudes how much he cares about his appearance. Wear fashionable clothing according to your style. If you like to wear sport coats, then wear them. If you like to wear nice jeans and a T-shirt, then wear those. Put on clothes that you feel confident in and show them off the best you can.

Hygiene:

A masculine man cares about how he looks and smells. Therefore, take showers regularly, keep your hair trimmed, cut your nails and brush your teeth.

Physical Activity:

This just means to take care of your body. You don't have to become a marathon runner or bodybuilder here. Just get up and start moving regularly. Whatever type of physical activity you want to engage in, do it on a regular basis.

Other Concepts of Masculinity

This final section of the chapter will be devoted to concepts related to masculinity that I have not gone over or want to reinforce further. After all this is said and done, you will know what it takes to be masculine, and therefore, a true alpha male.

Actions Speak Louder Than Words:

> *"Your actions speak so loudly, I cannot hear what you're saying."*
> - Ralph Waldo Emerson

People do a lot of talking and bragging these days. It seems like that's all you hear. Well, talking is okay if you want to explain something, but if you want to get things done, then you must start taking action. There's no way around it.

It is so easy nowadays to tell the world about our aspirations. There is very little accountability to make sure these aspirations happen and, therefore, no one takes any real actions. The ones who do, are the people getting things done. How many times do you get on social media and tell everyone that you want to travel, get a new job, start a business or have a family, then do nothing to make any of this happen?

The people reading your posts often don't live near you or by the time 10 minutes have passed, they've been inundated with many other posts and have forgotten about yours. Since you don't have to show your results, there is literally no accountability. You had no actual desire to do anything you spoke of. The praise you received was good enough.

True masculinity gives no credence to lip service. This means your words mean nothing if there is no action behind it. Real men take action to get things done. They talk less and work more, which is one of the reasons they are more successful. Remember that your potential, ideas and goals mean nothing if you do nothing about them.

So, the next time you catch yourself talking about losing weight, don't just go and sit on the couch. Go out and run around the block, pick up a dumbbell, start jumping rope or simply jog in place. Whatever idea you want to pursue, don't just think about it and then forget it existed. Start doing some actual work to get there. And don't whine about it!

Live Your Life Fearlessly:

Make yourself uncomfortable often and live life daringly. It is so easy for men to avoid discomfort these days. If they are hot, they can instantly cool down by turning on an air conditioner. If you don't have a car and don't want to walk a few blocks, then you can order an Uber. If you're hungry, just order through DoorDash or GrubHub. Life has become so convenient that men have become weaker. I can only imagine what would happen if the electrical grid went down and we would all have to fend for ourselves again.

There is an old saying that tough times create strong men; strong men create good times; good times create weak men; weak men create tough times. It seems like we are headed towards tough times eventually. I am not discrediting progress here. These modern conveniences were created by great men and women throughout history. Unfortunately, they have come with unintended consequences.

This is something we have to fight against a little bit. I am not asking you to go back to the Stone Ages here. I also take part in the comforts of the world and there's no denying that advancements have created a lot of opportunity. However, to be a strong man, you need to feel challenged on a regular basis. With challenge, comes discomfort. Hence, make yourself uncomfortable in life.

The following are some examples of discomfort you can create. These activities will make you grow and become stronger.

- Take a cold shower.
- Drive around for a few minutes in hot weather without air conditioning.
- Lift a heavy item once in a while.
- Walk to the store instead of driving or calling an Uber.
- Practice some fasting.
- Give up something you usually can't live without for a couple of days.

In summary, find ways to push yourself beyond your limits once in a while. Create some challenging circumstances that are not easy to overcome. You will begin to thank yourself when you have to face a challenge and it's not your choice.

Be unreasonable:

"The reasonable man adapts himself to the world; the unreasonable one persists in trying to adapt the world to himself. Therefore, all progress depends on the unreasonable man."

- George Bernard Shaw

From the time you were born, you have been taught to be a reasonable person. You were told not to ask too much of people, to follow the sure path to success via college, to be a good boy and follow the rules all the time. It's no wonder so many men cannot think for themselves and are unwilling to rock the boat.

People in our society are expected to adapt to the environment around them. This is okay for some, but they will just end up getting lost in the crowd. With true masculinity, a man is not interested in what society is like. He is interested in creating his own reality. As a result, he will not bend to the will of society, but make society bend to his desires. This does not mean he will force others to do things for him. However, he will use certain aspects of his environment as an advantage for him.

Living the status quo, 9-to-5 job, then coming home and watching TV is not what the masculine man desires. He wants more out of life and will figure out a way to get it. If you want to be more masculine, then start being unreasonable. Do not just go to work day after day because people tell you to. If you would rather live in a cabin deep in the woods or in a condo in New York City, instead of a house with a white picket fence, then do it. Make society be okay with your life. Don't build your life to please society.

Always Stay Grounded:

The true measure of a man is not keeping his cool when things are going well, but staying calm even when all hell breaks loose. To become a masculine man, you must remain grounded amidst any type of chaos going on. Losing your cool will not solve anything. This may sound antiquated, but during times of great distress, people still look for a strong male presence.

Most modern-day men fall apart when faced with adversity. They hide and run for cover. The few that don't are the real alpha males in our world. The problem is that weak men are completely controlled by their emotions. As a result, they give in to their impulses and run when there is danger.

Masculine men feel the same emotions as other men, they just do not give in to them. They remain grounded because they remember their true values in life. Always remember that no matter what chaos is going on in your life, you must keep your composure, because you can make it through.

There is no hidden secret to being a masculine man or an alpha male. It is actually quite simple. You just have to do things that other men are unwilling to do. These things are usually hard and create great resistance. Whether it's a personal goal, a work project or a chance to show your leadership in your community, many men in our comfortable world choose to avoid them. They avoid anything that challenges them and they no longer grow because of it.

Many of the strongest and most valuable commodities are made through extreme adversity. Diamonds are made under extreme heat and pressure. The hottest fires also create the strongest steel. The toughest of times create the strongest men. If you want to become a strong man, stop avoiding the difficult things in life. Choose the hard way instead of the easy way. When you make yourself tough, then good times are bound to follow and you will appreciate them more.

Chapter 6:

Confidence and Leadership

As we enter the final chapter of this book, I will discuss two separate qualities that any alpha male must possess -- confidence and leadership. I will discuss both of these concepts separately as they carry equal importance.

Confidence has been a major theme already throughout this book, as it is a staple of any alpha male that has existed throughout history. Think back and remember some of the confident men in your life. It does not even have to be someone you know. What common traits did these individuals carry? I imagine they had a certain aura about them, as if to say, "I am who I am, whether you like it or not." They probably weren't staring at the ground, fidgeting with their hands or trying to blend in. They carried themselves as a man should.

This is not done by accident. Self-assured men are not just born oozing confidence. They had to develop over time through practice and discipline. For those of you who weren't lucky enough to learn it, I will be showing it to you right now.

You're probably wondering if you are a confident man already. Well, if you have to ask, then you are not. You would not care about mine or anyone else's opinions. So, we have already established that we need to work on this. In all seriousness, though, there are certain attributes that a confident person has.

- He is not afraid to ask for what he wants.
- He is not bothered by the opinions of others.
- He has faith in himself to complete a project or task.
- He will admit when he does not know something.
- He has good posture.

- If he does not like something, he will let you know.
- He speaks with assertiveness.

I covered assertiveness in great detail in Chapter 3, so I will not rehash all of it here. I will say that assertiveness and confidence go hand in hand and you cannot have one without the other.

Confidence By Category

The thing about confidence is that it is very situational. This means we may be confident in one area of our lives, but lack it in other aspects. For example, when it comes to our jobs, we might know everything inside and out and be able to approach any situation confidently. If we go out to work on our car and don't have any automotive experience, then we probably will have less confidence in what we are doing. The goal is to have confidence in as many areas of life as possible, and if you are faced with a new situation, you at least have the ability to figure out a solution. This is kind of a "fake it till you make it" approach.

Confidence can be broken down even further into external and internal kinds.

External Confidence:

External confidence comes from competence. Basically, you become unafraid once you figure out what you are doing. Going back to the car example, once you understand the inner workings of the engine and get some actual training, you will gain more confidence in working on it. This can be relatable to any other area of your life as well. When you first started at your job, you probably did not feel too comfortable there until you got some experience. In relation to picking up women, the more you talk to them the easier it becomes. In any aspect of your life, external confidence increases once your competence rises in each type of situation.

Here are some scenarios to further explain external confidence.

- A man is comfortable on the construction site because he has worked there for years. When he tries to mingle at the nightclub, he just feels awkward.
- A man is confident when he bowls because he has been doing it since high school. When he tries to fix the plumbing in his house, he has no idea what he's doing because he has no experience in it.
- A man can solve any math problem in the world, but cannot understand Shakespeare for the life of him.

So, really, the way to gain external confidence is to become competent in whatever you are striving for.

Internal Confidence:

You can have huge amounts of internal confidence whether you have competence in anything or not. Studies have shown that if you portray yourself as a confident man, even if you are not well-versed in the particular subject matter, people still have more trust in you. For example, if two men are discussing economic policy and one of them is well educated on the subject, but appears meek, while the other one is not well educated on it but displays confidence, people will have more faith in what the second man says. This truly shows the power of internal confidence and why it is critical to develop yours.

You have probably known many guys who can speak confidently on just about any subject. It seems like whatever topic gets brought up, they have a strong opinion about it. This is the mark of internal confidence. If you carry this quality, you will seem more competent to most people, no matter how little your knowledge actually is.

A University of California, Berkeley study actually showed that people have more trust in those who seemed more naturally confident. They paid more attention to how a person carried themselves when they spoke, more so than the actual substance of their words. The same study showed that the confident individuals were more successful in achieving their goals, despite what their information base was.

While some men seem to be more confident naturally, it is actually a learned trait that anyone can pick up. So if you lacked internal confidence your whole life, you can still develop it now.

This power rests in the central belief that you can handle any problem or issue that shows up in your life, even if you have not been faced with it before. Once you have this mindset, then you are truly confident in your life. You will be a level above the anxious guys. The following are a few action steps you can start taking to increase your confidence now.

- First of all, adopt the belief I just mentioned above. You can handle anything that comes your way.
- Pick up as many skills as you can. The more you learn, the more confidence you will build, both externally and internally. Success in life gives confidence levels a big boost.
- Determine the areas of your life where you feel unsure of yourself. Then try doing the same things with more resolve. It's that simple. Just believe in yourself more when performing a task.
- Always be willing to try new things. Confidence and skill start to decrease when you become stagnant. Try something new and if you succeed, great. If you fail, you learn. It's a win-win situation.

Gaining confidence is about feeling better about yourself and living with less anxiety. Furthermore, people around you will feel more comfortable too. Think about the people you have worked with during your life. Whether the person was a doctor, lawyer, accountant, contractor or mechanic, you probably felt more at ease when they explained a situation calmly and clearly. Realize that other people feel that same way about you. So, if people seem uneasy when you're around, it might have something to do with the vibes you're putting out there. If you are still unsure about how to gain confidence, don't worry. I will provide more action steps later in this chapter.

Living as a Confident Man

You have probably figured out by now that confident men, like alpha males, live differently than the average man. They have more success, fun and memories. Confident men just see the world differently and, therefore, have different experiences. Some men sit around and wish they could be more confident. Others go out and become this way. You need to start becoming confident too and not just wonder about it.

Have a Vision:

A confident man has a vision about his future and he is determined to make it a reality. Whether it is a career, house, partner or financial status, he knows what he wants out of life. Through turmoil, setbacks and various negative experiences, the confident man never loses his focus. It is burned into his memory and, despite the obstacles that come up, he figures out a way to reach his goals. It is just part of who he is.

You may be wondering how you develop a vision for your own life. Well, the main thing to remember is that it's yours and no one can decide it for you. You know yourself better than anyone else, so come up with something based on your strongest desires. To help you out a little, here are a few suggestions.

- Write down what you want for your future and be as descriptive as you can about it.
- Review your old dreams and goals. Determine if they are still relevant or need to be discarded for newer dreams. People change their minds throughout their lives, even alpha males. It's part of learning and growing.
- Start coming up with small steps to make your vision a reality. This will also help you realize what is practical at the current moment.
- Your vision does not have to be carved in stone. Feel free to grow and expand on it as you also grow as a person.
- Never be ashamed of your vision. There are plenty of people who were laughing stocks before they made their dreams a reality and reached the next level.
- Revisit your goals frequently to make sure you are on the right track.

Once you have a solid vision, you will become more confident about your future. We are just starting to plant the seeds, so let's keep going.

Get to Know Yourself:

Confident men know themselves well. Imagine for a moment that you are in the middle of a project, whether at home or at work. Suddenly, a friend walks up and asks you why you're doing something a certain way. Once you receive this question, your reaction will say a lot about your confidence level. If you are assured in your skills, then you will not be fazed by your friend's question. You will be able to answer it quickly then get back to work. Or, you can simply tell them that you know what you are doing and ignore them. If you are insecure, then you will react with anger or confusion.

The bottom line is that you will know who you are and what you're capable of. If you are one to question yourself and your skillset easily, then you have some room to let your confidence grow. Here are a few tips to help you get to know yourself.

- Start putting in the work to get better. The more you practice something, the more skilled and confident you will become.
- Reflect on what you know and don't know. What are your strengths and weaknesses? Be completely honest with yourself. This will give you the confidence to know what you are and are not capable of.
- Ask your friends what they view as your strengths and weaknesses too. Put the same question to several people to get an all-around view. You will also start seeing patterns in what people say.
- Personality tests are a good way to get an assessment of yourself and figure out why you think the way you do.

Take Action:

I covered this a lot in the previous chapter, but to reiterate the point, confident men do, they do not just wonder. He feels the same fear and anxiety that others do, but he doesn't let these emotions overtake him. He doesn't allow his fears hold him back, while the insecure man will.

Take action on a daily basis, just like a confident man and you will soon be that type of man. Taking action continuously helps you understand that anxiety can't control you if you don't let it. Soon, you will develop the natural skill to keep pushing through negative emotions. The following are some practical steps to improve your ability to take action.

- Make your bed every morning. This is a first action step to get your day in order and gets you in the habit of getting things done.
- Have a workout routine that you do every day.

- Force yourself to do something you don't want to do on a regular basis.
- When you feel anxious or fearful, ask yourself why and see if you can push through it. Often, the fear of something happening is worse than it actually happening.
- Create daily tasks for you to complete every day and cross them off the list as you do to create a sense of accomplishment.

Do not overwhelm yourself with unrealistic expectations. Having confidence will give you the ability to get more done, but it won't make you superhuman. Break large tasks down into simpler and achievable steps.

Be Okay With Failing:

Many high-level achievers boast about how they are successful in life because they were not afraid to fail. Fear of failure is a real thing and it stops people from achieving their goals in a major way. However, if you have never fallen short at anything, then you have not tried enough things. In order to gain confidence, you need to become okay with failing, otherwise, the crippling fear will always exist. The more you try and sometimes fail, the easier it will become. You will eventually be able to stomach it. The key is to also learn from it, otherwise, it was a wasted effort.

Men who become okay with failing break the cycle of shame that holds them back. They stop caring about looking badly and just keep moving forward. Failure is never fun, but it is essential for growth. The following are some ways that a misstep can become easier to take.

- If you are afraid of failure, ask yourself why you are scared. Often, you cannot come up with a legitimate answer, so the power gets disarmed.
- Practice failing at things and you will become better at getting over it. Force yourself to do things you are not good at or have

never done. Soon, you will be failing like a champ and learning from those experiences.

Confident Men Take Care of Themselves:

You probably have not met too many confident men who were grossly overweight, dressed poorly or had bad hygiene. The reason for this is because self-assured men take the time to care for themselves. They work out regularly, eat the right foods, pay close attention to hygiene and have a nice wardrobe that fits them. Self-confident men value themselves, so they take the time for self-care. The following are a few steps to start taking care of yourself today.

- Brush your teeth twice a day; fix your hair; keep your nails trimmed; and make sure to take a shower regularly, especially after workouts.
- Research better and healthier diet options for you that make you feel energized. What you eat plays a big role in your mood later on. This is not just due to weight loss and health, but also overall energy levels.
- Pursue hobbies that you are passionate about. It can be anything from ceramics to scuba diving.
- Work on ways to get out of a toxic environment, whether at home or at work.

Once you start taking care of yourself regularly, it will become a habit. You will begin putting it at the forefront of your routine.

Push Your Boundaries:

Confident men do not stay within their comfort zones. They push their limits constantly, which helps them grow. This could mean growing their business, running an extra mile in the morning, going somewhere they've never been or talking to someone they've never met. Whatever the case, you cannot grow your confidence if you are not willing to push the boundaries on a regular basis.

Pushing yourself is not easy. You just have to start doing it no matter the pain or suffering it causes. Those discomforts are temporary, but the results are everlasting. Of course you want to be reasonable with your progress. If you bench-press 225 pounds, don't just move up to 325 pounds the next day. That is not confidence, it's just stupidity. The following are some tips to help you start challenging your limits.

- When you start feeling uncomfortable, do not stop. Keep pushing a little bit harder.
- Perform your difficult tasks first while you still have energy.
- Focus on certain areas of your life at a time when trying to challenge yourself. Don't try to do all of it at once.
- Assess where you have come from and the growth you have already made. Now, use this as motivation for continued growth.

Think Positively:

This may seem obvious, but it is also imperative. Confident men have to think in positive terms about themselves and their futures. They focus on things that will be beneficial to them and do not let the negative aspects of life control them. For example, while out for a run, a man might start getting tired, sore and thirsty and want to quit. He acknowledges these negative aspects related to the run, but also knows that if he goes five or 10 more minutes, he will increase his strength and endurance. The following are a few practical tips to help you start focusing on positive things.

- Stop and realize you are focusing on something negative. If you feel stuck, assess where your thoughts are, then start shifting them appropriately to the end goal.

- When faced with a very challenging situation, think about and write down all of the positive things that will happen if you complete the task at hand.
- Regularly write down the positive things in your life and focus your attention on those.

Slowly, you will retrain your brain to think positively.

Be Generous:

Confident men are also generous. They know what they have to offer and are happy to give it when they can. Mind you, they do not just give things away wastefully. They will also make sure their needs are taken care of first. Here are some generosity tips to follow.

- With the extra money, find a non-profit to donate to. If you don't have the money, then you can always donate your valuable time.
- Seek out friends, family or neighbors that are struggling and find ways to help them too.
- Start small with your generosity and move up slowly as you feel comfortable.
- Be generous with the resources you can comfortably give, whether food, money, clothing or time.

Helping other people makes you feel good about yourself and increases your confidence. You will also get used to sharing your resources with genuine intent.

Ask Questions:

Confident men are not afraid to ask questions. This shows that you are not a know-it-all and are willing to learn new information. It also shows interest and engagement, and people will like you more for it. Asking questions is especially beneficial when you are having a conversation with someone you staunchly disagree with. This allows you to understand their point of view and it may help you think in a different manner too. Consider some of the following tips.

- Always ask for clarification on something you don't fully understand before responding with your own opinion. This will show that your response was thought through well.
- Rather than always answering with a statement, try asking more followup questions.
- Observe people's reactions to questions instead of statements and how they differ.

Get used to asking questions instead of always having all the answers.

Don't be a People Pleaser:

A man of confidence knows when people around him need help and he is happy to give it to them when he can. However, he is not a people pleaser. He does not go completely out of his way to placate someone, especially when it is at his own expense. The confident man is okay with not being popular. He likes himself and that is good enough for him.

The following are some ways to stop being a people pleaser.

- Self-audit and determine if you are changing your thoughts, beliefs and values so you don't upset anyone else. If so, this is a big red flag. You don't have to get into arguments about your views, but don't be vocal about them unless you are willing to stick by them too.
- Next time you are around someone you dislike, ask yourself why. Is it necessary for you to be near them at that moment?

- As always, learn to say "no." It is a powerful word, especially when you say it with purpose.

The only person you are required to please is yourself. Everyone else can learn to please themselves.

These are just a few obvious traits related to confident men. There are many more. The bottom line is, a confident man believes in himself, will learn to solve problems critically because he knows he can, is kind to others but not a pushover, is always ready to learn, and is focused on his future. The confident man will not tell you who he is, but you will know he is someone special. He will have a presence about himself.

If this sounds appealing to you, then that's good. The goal is to make you a confident man too, with similar traits like I have described.

Becoming a Confident Man

Now that I have described the many attributes of a confident man, it is time to take the proper action steps to become one yourself. Each technique we go over will have its own unique way of building your confidence. After practicing all of them, you will place a high value on yourself because you will know you are worth it.

10 Tips to Higher Self-Confidence and Self-Esteem:

Most men struggle to build their confidence because they don't really know how. They have been beaten down by life and its circumstances over and over again. Believing in themselves becomes like a long-lost fantasy. It is actually easier than you think to rebuild your confidence and I will show you through 10 easy-to-follow steps.

1) **Believe in Your Ability to Make Good Decisions:**

You do not have to seek out answers from other people about decisions that affect your life. It's one thing to ask for advice. It's another thing to let someone come up with solutions for you. To build your self-confidence and self-esteem, you must start believing in yourself that you can set the course for your life. You can because you know yourself better than anyone else.

Mindfulness is a great technique for getting yourself in the present moment and focusing on the task at hand. Affirm to yourself that you have the background, knowledge and experience to make appropriate decisions for you. Before you can go any further, you must get this step down.

Just so you know, you will make mistakes. Everyone makes them and it's not the end of the world. The good thing is that the mistakes will be yours, so you can learn from them and move forward.

2) Shield Yourself From Negativity:

To make proper decisions, you must also be able to tune out negativity. Any words that undermined your confidence in the past must be shielded from your mind. This included the negative stuff you said or thought about yourself. It will not do you any good now. Be aware of your past so you can learn from it, but keep your eye on the future.

3) Embrace Your Mistakes:

I mentioned this in tip one, but it's important to note that mistakes will be made along the way. You can either run from them or learn from them. Take solace in the fact that the mistakes are yours, which means you are at least trying to make progress. When you make a mistake, ask yourself what lessons you can take from it.

4) Focus on Your Positive Assets:

When taking stock of your life, it is very easy to start thinking about the things that are absent in your life. What about the assets, though? That is what you should be focusing on. Confident men don't worry about what they don't have. They pay attention to their physical, personal and intellectual assets and become grateful for them. They also start working towards what they want in the future. List your own assets now and do this regularly.

5) Practice Gratitude:

This goes along the lines of the previous tip. We all have something to be grateful for in life and these are things we should appreciate. This has a direct effect on your self-esteem. Always ask yourself what you are grateful for. Keep a list and continue adding to it. Gratitude is a great contributor to humility.

6) Change Your Mental Tape:

Changing the voice in your head means that you adjust your self-speak. If you find yourself always talking negatively while standing in front of a mirror, then you have negative mental tape and need to change it. Start focusing on your positive attributes and telling yourself about those in the mirror. Trust me, you have plenty.

7) Accept Change:

Change is inevitable and also constant. A confident man knows this and accepts it. Even if he doesn't like it, he does not whine about it. He makes the proper adjustments and uses change to his advantage, whether it is related to his career or personal life. A self-confident man knows that he is always changing too. If you are going to evolve anyway, then you might as well be for the better. The question to ask yourself is: What positive changes are you making in your life? I hope you're focusing on the aspects of your life that need improvement.

8) Believe that You Are Worthy of Happiness:

Confident men take their own happiness seriously. They realize it is a necessity and will put it at the forefront of their minds. In order to attract success, happiness and anything else good in your life, you must believe you are worthy of it. Put any thoughts that state you aren't worthy of being happy completely out of your mind. This goes back to the Law of Attraction where you only focus on what you actually want.

9) **Engage in Self-Care:**

I have already spoken about this several times, so I won't get into it too much here. Just always take care of yourself in every respect, physically, mentally and emotionally because you deserve it.

10) **Embrace Your Imperfections:**

Everybody has flaws. Most people are ashamed of them, but men who are confident embrace them. Realize that many people out there probably share the same imperfections as you. Assess your own and determine if they are really that bad. Also, figure out if anything can be gained from your perceived shortcomings. In this respect, they become a gift in disguise.

Men who are confident heavily believe in these 10 concepts described above. They have fully accepted who they are, which means they have no problems looking someone in the eye. They also know who they want to become and will figure out how to get where they want to be.

Confident men, like alpha males in general, attract other people to them because of their magnetic personalities. They do not act like they need people, because deep down, they don't. In addition to people, you will also attract more money, better health and success, in general. It will come to you because you know you are worthy of it.

What Confident Men Don't Do:

By now, you can probably figure out much of this list on your own. However, it is important to go over several things that confident men don't do. It is very unbecoming of them and if you find yourself doing any of these, I urge you to stop right away. Even if you practice the tips from the previous section, if you engage in these acts, you will still be held back from gaining full confidence and self-esteem. I will provide another list of 10 things to consider.

1) Do Not Wear Flashy Bands or Logos:

This is just a way to show off and does not showcase any type of style or taste. Basically, you are just telling people you have money to spend and confident men do not waste time showing off. People often wear these designs to make others jealous. There is really nothing appealing about wearing flashy bands or logos. It just shows you have a lack of confidence so don't wear them.

2) Do Not Dress Inappropriately for an Occasion:

Basically, do not wear tank tops to a wedding and don't wear a tuxedo to play basketball. I know these are ridiculous examples but are there to prove a point. While a confident man is not afraid to wear what he wants when he wants, there is still a time and a place for appropriate clothing. Be aware of the times that your fashion taste may need to take a backseat.

A confident man is never purposefully disrespectful, and having inappropriate clothing can send that message in certain instances. This is mainly because it puts all the attention on you and takes it away from the others. This can be especially controversial at a wedding or funeral.

3) Do Not Do Things Simply to Look Successful:

There is a difference between looking successful and actually being successful. Buying an expensive car, house, watch or another material possession that you can't afford is just poor money management. It does not make you confident in any way. As a matter of fact, it makes you less so, because you are obsessed with impressing people.

Look at some of the wealthiest people out there, like Mark Zuckerberg or Bill Gates, and notice that they aren't wearing the most expensive clothing or Rolex watches. They don't need to show you how rich they are. Don't live outside your means to impress people. Be happy with where you are and work towards getting where you want to be. In the future, if you want to buy expensive things, do it for your own pride and not to show off.

4) Do Not Fear Being Judged Unfairly:

A confident man is happy with where he is. Other people will not feel the same way. No matter who you are, people are going to assess you without really getting to know you. This is a harsh reality of life. They will judge you for your clothes, where you live, your career choices, and how you decide to live your life. If you are confident, these judgments will not phase you. You will continue living your life in a way that makes you happy. So, wear that funky hat if you want, go to the arcade even if you're an adult and spend your weekends doing as you please because other people's opinions do not matter.

5) Do Not Constantly Come Up With Excuses:

When you make an excuse, you are taking the blame off of yourself. Sometimes, excuses are valid. If you are supposed to meet a friend at 5 p.m., and all the roads become jammed suddenly, then it is out of your control and you have an acceptable reason to be late. Just don't make this a pattern. If you are late all the time, you are just inconsiderate or have poor time-management skills.

When you create a pattern of excuses, it shows you take no responsibility and nothing is ever your fault. This means you are ignoring your shortcomings, and confident people never do that. They realize their faults and try to correct them. If you always make excuses, other people will take notice and start losing respect for you.

6) Do Not Wait for Permission to Act:

If you are an adult, you do not have a mommy or daddy your need to check in with. Do whatever actions you think are right for your life and do not wait for permission to proceed. This also means not waiting for recognition that you are good enough to follow your dreams. If you feel that you are good enough, then you are good enough. That is all you really need to take the next step.

7) Do Not Fear Feedback or Inconvenient Truths:

You are not perfect, and people will often tell you so. That is okay because this can be a major learning experience. Do not fear feedback or the truth, even if it's negative. Assess what people are telling you, determine the validity then learn from it. Avoiding these things is just another example of not taking responsibility. You will never grow if you are never willing to accept any feedback.

8) Do Not Yield to Peer Pressure:

Once again, we are not in high school, so stop living to satisfy others. When you give in to peer pressure, you are going against what you want to do and making other people happy in the process. A confident man will speak up and refuse to do something he does not want to do, despite what people will think about it. You are your own person who is quite capable of doing the right thing for you for the right reasons, regardless of your friends' opinions. If they are true friends, they will support you.

9) Do Not Hide Behind Screens:

It is very easy to remain anonymous these days and get away with saying whatever you want. You don't even have to put up a profile picture, so no one will really know who you are. Hiding behind a mirage just shows that you are afraid to stand behind what you say. If you feel like you have to hide while you say something, then you probably should not say it in the first place.

10) Do Not Fear Asking for Help if You Need It:

Everybody needs help sometimes. A confident man will know when he's over his head and won't hesitate to ask for help. In order to build your life along the way, you are going to need to rely on other people. The sooner you are ready to accept this fact, the easier it will be.

I urge you to stop doing all of these immediately because they are off-putting. Based on the descriptions I have gone over, if you find yourself doing things that go against the qualities of a confident man or alpha male, in general, then work on improving those too. Being confident is not just about what you do, but what you don't do, as well.

Here's an exercise that might help. Every time you start taking one of these actions, *stop* what you're doing, step back, and take a deep breath. Figure out why you are about to go down this route, then change directions. This requires self-consciousness. You must be aware of yourself at all times and soon enough, it will become a habit. Good luck!

Finding the Leader Within You

A man is not given the title of a leader, it is something that is earned through words and actions. A leader inspires and motivates people to become their best selves. A leader does not openly chastise or ridicule someone when they've made a mistake. They help the person acknowledge and learn when they err so that they can do better the next time. A leader does not just tell people what to do. He shows them by example. Knowing he has their back, they strive to perform to a higher standard.

A leader is confident enough to not showboat when he's been successful and humble enough to admit when he has made a mistake. He is a man of few words and of massive action. To earn the respect of a leader, you must be honest, hardworking and motivated. As you can see, the true qualities of leadership come from being a confident man. Without confidence, you will be a weak leader who has no authority or respect from those who are supposedly following you. The good news in this regard is that a weak leader will not have followers for very long, because they will leave him quickly.

Without confidence, there is no leadership, because this quality is the foundation of being an effective leader. The following are a few reasons why:

- As a leader, you will make important decisions that will impact many people. You will have to be confident in them, even if other people question you.
- You will need to communicate with assertiveness, which means clearly and confidently.
- You will need to be great at developing relationships.
- People need to trust you and they won't if you are weak. Would you want to follow someone who doesn't even know where he's going?
- You will fail plenty of times and you need to be okay with that.
- You will have to take significant risks, which will require a lot of faith in yourself.
- You will have plenty of haters, and you cannot let them get under your skin.

These factors are not exclusive to running a business or corporation. They relate to every part of your life. It is important to be the leader in your life too because the path you take will affect you the most.

What Makes a Leader?:

Once you start becoming a confident man and an alpha male, you will become a leader, whether you intend to or not. People will be drawn to your strength and notice your positive leadership qualities. As a result, they will turn to you for guidance, no matter what situation they are in. In this section, I will discuss what being a leader is and the qualifications required.

First of all, some people equate being a leader to being a boss, manager or some other authoritative role. However, as I stated at the beginning, leadership is not given or appointed to someone. Therefore, a boss is not automatically a leader. Just as a note, many individuals achieve the role of boss or manager because of their leadership skills, but the point here is that one does not necessarily equate to the other.

Leadership also is not dependent on your education or training. You cannot go to school and then just learn how to become a leader. You can learn principles and start applying them in practical settings, but you cannot just assume that the higher a person's educational background, the more effective they will be. By the way, that is exactly what we are doing here. I cannot make you a leader, but I can show you the steps you can take. Before we get there, though, let's go over some of the key attributes of being a real leader.

- Being honest and trustworthy. There is no way around this one. A leader must conduct himself with dignity. Whether he's right or wrong, he must be upfront about it.
- He must be a great communicator. I spoke about assertive communication in Chapter 3. This strategy is imperative in communicating effectively. This does not just mean being good at talking. You must actually make a point and get it across.
- You must be clear, concise and organized. This deals with effective communication and the proper actions that follow. If you do not display all three of these traits, then you and those around you will have no idea what to do.
- You need to be decisive, but also flexible. You will need to make tough decisions based on the information you know at hand, but also be ready to switch things up as more information comes out or if things are not going as planned.
- You need to be passionate in everything you are involved with. This will help inspire and motivate people. Passion is infectious and if you don't possess it, people will not take you seriously.
- Any good leader will look for the right tools to get the job done efficiently. This is needed to streamline many processes, which is essential because you only have a certain number of hours in a day. A leader has great time-management skills.

Wow! It's like I just regurgitated the information about being confident. Well, not really, but it just goes to show you that confidence and leadership are closely related. Once you increase your confidence level, you are on your way to becoming a great leader. Of course, there are still a few steps you need to take. You can also become a confident bad leader, so you need to hone your skills. In the next section, I will go over how to further train your leadership skills.

Learn Leadership:

To end this book, I will go over some techniques you can start doing to help build your leadership skills. Remember, though, to engage in these practices, you must already have some self-confidence. If you are not there yet, then keep practicing before you engage in these final steps. Many of the theories and practices I have already gone over in this book, like assertive communication, can be used in leadership training. Now, let's start honing your skills.

Practice Being Honest:

Practice being honest all the time. Even for the little things that may not matter much, still be honest. Some people avoid being candid to spare someone's feelings, such as when they cook something that does not taste right, but they don't have the heart to tell them. Believe me, I totally understand. But to become a fully honest person, you must be okay with hurting someone's feelings and even offending them. so, practice honesty in every way. You don't have to be rude about it, but definitely straightforward.

If you are eating something that was cooked by another person and it does not come out right, then let them know. If someone does something that turns you off, let them know. Be honest in your approach with every situation in your life and you will slowly build up your tolerance.

Delegate and Prioritize Tasks:

A good leader knows he cannot accomplish everything on his own. This is why he must surround himself with good people. He must also determine the most critical tasks to be completed and prioritize those.

To delegate tasks properly, you must understand the strengths and weaknesses of your team, so that the correct tasks can be assigned. Your team members must also be comfortable coming up to you if they are not able to do something. After determining the most important tasks of the day, make sure they are completed first, either by you or someone else who is qualified.

Communicate Constantly:

It is not just important to have effective communication, but also constant communication. If you communicate effectively once in a while, it won't be very productive. Therefore, the communication needs to be done frequently to make sure everyone is on the same page. Communication does not always have to be face-to-face. Emails, phone calls and Zoom meetings are acceptable too. Just make sure your presence is felt. The last thing you want is for your team to think you bailed on them.

Commit Yourself:

Commit yourself to become a great leader. Always be willing to learn new things and keep improving your skills. Great leaders never stop growing and learning, whether it is by reading books constantly, talking to other leaders or doing frequent self-assessments.

Think Creatively:

It can be easy to follow the same course of action all the time, however, sometimes this is what led to certain problems in the first place. To be able to solve a new set of problems that comes your way, you will have to start thinking creatively. This will allow you to come up with a new set of solutions.

Lead With Positivity:

As a leader, the people around you will basically follow your act. This means they will mimic your contagious mood. So, if you are anxious, frustrated and impatient, everyone else will be too. Learn to transform all of your negative emotions into something positive. Also have a proactive approach in your work, which will show your team how to push through tough times.

Follow Your Intuition:

While you can take all of the advice, guidance and thought processes of other people, each decision you make will ultimately be on you. This is why it is important to trust your intuition. After you have whatever information you can collect at the time, the decision you make afterward will require a certain amount of faith. The results will never be certain, which is why you need to trust your gut. If you have a good or bad feeling inside of you, learn to listen to it.

Tailor Your Approach:

As a leader, you will be working with different types of people. There are all sorts of courses and training out there that teach you how to deal with people. However, each person requires a different approach. Some individuals learn from a hardline approach, while others benefit from softer methods. This is why it's important to understand your followers and their needs. Tailor your approach to handling specific situations based on the people involved.

It all starts with confidence, and from there, you can hone in on specific aspects of your personality to develop your leadership skills. You have come this far and you are now ready to be a confident alpha male and leader.

Conclusion

I want to thank you for reading my book, *The Modern Alpha Male: A Guide to Masculinity, Women, Money, Assertiveness and Success*. My hope is that you enjoyed the content while also getting some valuable information. I am pained by the fact that real men have been so demonized in our society. What makes it worse is that it is based on several falsehoods. The goal of this book was to describe the true qualities of an alpha male so that other men out there won't be ashamed of being one, and women will stop believing the lie that masculinity is toxic. It is not and I have proven it in this book.

I have covered many different topics and subtopics in this book, but they all center around being a well-rounded alpha male. If you want any type of success in your life, whether it is a career, money, women, health or relationships, then you must possess the qualities of this type of man. True success comes from living the life you want, and not the one society thinks you should have. To live this way, you must not be afraid to bring out your inner alpha.

As I went through the chapters of this book, I started by thoroughly describing the alpha male to immediately clear up any misconceptions. Following this, I got into depth about the risks of being a "nice guy" and how it can be counterintuitive to being a good man. A common theme throughout this book is that the negative traits attributed to alpha males are actually more in line with the opposite kind of man, namely beta and omega males. Therefore the reason so many people are put off my alphas is that they have fallen for the lies that are out there. I have uncovered those falsehoods in this book, so you can see for yourself how unfairly real men have been treated in the modern era.

The remainder of this book provides many tips and strategies on how to stop being weak and start living your life with purpose and intensity. Assertiveness, confidence and positivity are all foundational principles in manhood and these topics have been covered in-depth throughout the various chapters. The book ends with going over what an alpha male naturally becomes, whether he is assigned the position or not, and that is a true leader. People are attracted to alpha males like magnets, therefore, look to them for guidance and strength.

After reading this book, I hope you are a proud man who is not ashamed of his alpha-male qualities. Remember that the strategies I went over in this book should be utilized throughout your life. This is not just a book, but a reference manual. Refer back to it often. Being a real man is hard work and takes continuous practice. Never stop growing.

The next step is to take the information from this book and apply it to your own life. The sooner you start, the quicker your life will begin to turn around. Start becoming the alpha male you are supposed to be. The world needs more men like you. Once again, thank you for taking the time to read this book. I want as many people as possible to benefit from it, so if you enjoyed the content, a review on Amazon would be greatly appreciated.

References

10 Steps to Help you Become a Successful Leader. (2017, June 16). www.Kangan.Edu.Au. https://www.kangan.edu.au/students/blog/become-a-successful-leader

25 Characteristics of an Alpha Male. (2012, November 1). Chadhowsefitness.Com. http://chadhowsefitness.com/2012/11/25-characteristics-of-an-alpha-male/

Bacon, D. (n.d.-b). Alpha Male vs. Beta Male: What's the Difference? | The Modern Man. www.themodernman.com. Retrieved July 12, 2020, from https://www.themodernman.com/success/alpha-male-vs-beta-male.html

Bailey, S. (2018, May 23). *A psychological review of the 'Nice Guy.'* Medium. https://medium.com/@supersonny68/a-psychological-review-of-the-nice-guy-92c86e6aa752

Busch, J. (2012, July 2). *Don't Be a Dick: The False Virtues of the Classic Alpha Male.* Primer. https://www.primermagazine.com/2012/live/dont-be-a-dick-the-false-virtues-of-the-classic-alpha-male

Campbell, S. (2018, August 30). *How to Stop Being a Nice Guy and Start Living the Life You Deserve.* Unstoppable Rise. https://www.unstoppablerise.com/nice-guy-syndrome/

Canfield, J. (2019, January 2). *Using the Law of Attraction for Joy, Relationships, Money & More [Guide].* America's Leading

Authority On Creating Success And Personal Fulfillment - Jack Canfield. https://www.jackcanfield.com/blog/using-the-law-of-attraction/

Chua, C. (2014, June 8). *7 Tips to Choose Your Battles and Fight for What Matters*. Personal Excellence. https://personalexcellence.co/blog/choose-your-battles/#

Confident Man: *10 Steps to Higher Self-Esteem* | Guy Counseling. (2014, October 7). Guy Counseling. https://guycounseling.com/confident-man-10-steps-to-higher-self-esteem/

Dao, F. (2008, March). *Without Confidence, There is No Leadership*. Inc.Com; Inc. https://www.inc.com/resources/leadership/articles/20080301/dao.html

Daskal, L. (2016, May 19). *7 Powerful Habits That Make You More Assertive*. Inc.Com; Inc. https://www.inc.com/lolly-daskal/7-powerful-habits-that-make-you-more-assertive.html

Dimas, J. (2020, January 17). *How to Use the Law of Attraction to Change Your Life*. Dwell in Magic. https://jessicadimas.com/how-to-effectively-use-the-law-of-attraction/

Eason, A. (2018, January 23). *Assertive: The importance of being so & why being assertive benefits you*. Adam Eason. https://www.adam-eason.com/assertive-assertiveness-importance/

Ferebee, A. (2019, September 17). *9 Powerful Alpha Male Traits You MUST Develop to Be Your Best Self*. Knowledge For Men. https://www.knowledgeformen.com/alpha-male-traits/

Ferebee, A. (2019, October 31). *[Ultimate Guide] How to Be More Masculine in a Hyper Feminine World*. Knowledge For Men. https://www.knowledgeformen.com/how-to-be-more-masculine/

Gray, J. (2017, March 25). *How To Develop Your Masculine Edge: 9 Steps To Becoming A Beast.* Jordan Gray Consulting. https://www.jordangrayconsulting.com/develop-your-masculine-edge-9-steps-to-becoming-a-beast/

Greater Minds. (n.d.). *What Is The Law Of Attraction? And How To Use It Effectively.* The Law Of Attraction. Retrieved July 21, 2020, from https://www.thelawofattraction.com/what-is-the-law-of-attraction/

Gurian, M. (2019, January 24). *Masculinity Is Not Our Enemy.* Psychology Today. https://www.psychologytoday.com/us/blog/the-minds-boys-and-girls/201901/masculinity-is-not-our-enemy

How to Increase Masculine Energy and Rebuild Self-Esteem | How to Beast. (n.d.). How to Beast. Retrieved July 23, 2020, from https://www.howtobeast.com/how-to-reclaim-your-manhood-and-rapidly-cultivate-masculine-energy/

How to be more Masculine Without Being A Total Jerk. (n.d.). LifeOS. Retrieved July 23, 2020, from https://lifeoperatingsystem.com/how-to-be-more-masculine/

Hurst, K. (2019, June 5). *Law Of Attraction History: The Origins Of The Law Of Attraction Uncovered.* The Law Of Attraction. https://www.thelawofattraction.com/history-law-attraction-uncovered/

Ludeman, K., & Erlandson, E. (n.d.). *The Alpha Male Syndrome - Synopsis.* www.Worthethic.Com. Retrieved July 11, 2020, from http://www.worthethic.com/the-alpha-male-syndrome.html?pg=AS_Summary

Mayo Clinic Staff. (2017). *Stressed out? Be assertive.* Mayo Clinic. https://www.mayoclinic.org/healthy-lifestyle/stress-management/in-depth/assertive/art-20044644

Pedersen, C. (2017, October 25). *Self-Confidence for Men: The Ultimate Guide*. ManTalks. https://mantalks.com/self-confidence-for-men/

Ramos, T. (2019, January 2). *How to Be a Leader: 6 Qualifications and Qualities*. Runrun.It Blog. https://blog.runrun.it/en/how-to-be-a-leader/

Richard. (2018, July 5). *Have You Got the Dreaded "Nice Guy Syndrome"?* Recovering Man. https://recoveringman.org/nice-guy-syndrome/

Schneider, S. R. (2019, August 16). *16 Things Confident Men Never Do - Confidence Boosters for Gentlemen — Gentleman's Gazette*. www.Gentlemansgazette.com. https://www.gentlemansgazette.com/confidence-boosters-for-gentlemen/

Simple ways to become more masculine. (2018, February 14). The Man Effect. http://themaneffect.com/thejourney/simple-ways-to-become-more-masculine

The Importance of Being Assertive. (n.d.). Teodesk. Retrieved July 20, 2020, from https://www.teodesk.com/blog/the-importance-of-being-assertive/

Wenger, T. (2018, March 25). *15 Ways You Can Become More Confident As A Man*. The Man Effect. http://themaneffect.com/thejourney/15-ways-you-can-become-more-confident-as-a-man

Wignall, N. (2019, March 15). *Assertiveness: A Step-by-Step Guide to Becoming More Assertive [2020]*. Nick Wignall. https://nickwignall.com/assertiveness/

Yugay, I. (2019, January 27). *The Complete Law of Attraction Guide: How To Manifest Your Dream Life*. Mindvalley Blog. https://blog.mindvalley.com/law-of-attraction/

Printed in Great Britain
by Amazon